SUBCHASER
IN THE
SOUTH PACIFIC

Subchaser
in the South Pacific

A Saga of the USS SC-761 During World War II

By J. Henry Doscher, Jr.
Captain, USNR (Ret.)

ibooks

DISTRIBUTED BY PUBLISHERS GROUP WEST

A publication of ibooks, inc.

Copyright © 1994, 2006 by J. Henry Doscher, Jr.

Distributed by Publishers Group West
1700 Fourth Street, Berkeley, CA 94710

An ibooks, inc. Book

ibooks, inc.
24 West 25th Street
New York, NY 10010

Published with permission by Eakin Press.

ISBN 1-59687-332-9
First ibooks, inc. printing February 2006

10 9 8 7 6 5 4 3 2 1

Printed in the U.S.A.

*This book is dedicated to
Jim Hannah, Don Terry and Joe Effinger,
agelong friends, without whose help and encouragement
this book would not have been possible.*

Contents

Acknowledgments

It has been my pleasure to have received the assistance and guidance of various persons, not the least of whom are many former members of ship's company on the USS *SC-761*.

I am greatly indebted to Mr. Richard A. von Doenhoff, Military Reference Branch, Textual Reference Division, National Archives, Washington, D.C., for his assistance regarding all types of available official records and charts.

To others who furnished data or made records available including: Dr. Dean C. Allard and Ms. Cathy Lloyd of the U.S. Naval Historical Center in the Washington Navy Yard, Washington, D.C.; Rear Adm. Norvell G. Ward, USN (Ret.), now of Atlantic Beach, Florida; Col. Herbert E. Halliday, USA (Ret.), now of Carlisle, Pennsylvania; Mr. Warner Keeley, Jr., now of Pebble Beach, California; Mr. Martin Clemens, former Solomon Islands coastwatcher, now of Dunraven, at Toorak, Victoria, Australia; Lt. Comdr. John R. Keenan, Royal Australian Navy (Ret.), now of Nambour, Queensland, Australia; and Ms. Natalie Anderson, reference librarian, Ipswich Public Library, Ipswich, Massachusetts.

To those who have proofread and critiqued my manuscript, especially Ms. Ruth H. Williamson, Ms. Gwen Choate Smith and Professor Patrick Bennett, each of Abilene, Texas.

To all of the above, I am forever grateful.

THE SPLINTER FLEET
By Oris E. Moore

They sing the praises of the battleship,
The carrier is Queen of the Sea;
The cruiser is tops on sailors' lists,
For fighting ship is she.

The destroyer sails the sea with pride,
The submarine's work is neat;
But we are the legion of forgotten men,
The sailors of the S.C. fleet.

We are indeed a motherless child,
A long, long way from home;
Our base is any port we make,
For our destiny is to roam.

No concern is shown for the work we do,
No thought for the way we live;
Like sardines packed in wooden crates,
Which generally leak like a sieve.

We bounce around like a piece of cork,
No rest is to be had at sea;
The duty is tough and never ends,
But the life we live is free.

Our chow all comes from box or can,
Nothing fresh ever comes our way;
We do our laundry in the propeller wash,
It's the system that is here to stay.

We comb our hair with a ki-yi brush,
Take showers in water from the sea;
Our one trademark is ruggedness,
Yes, a salty bunch are we.

Our stay in port is never long,
For we have much work to do;
We've forgotten the ease of civvy life,
And are happy where the water is blue.

Wooden ships and iron men,
Are a tradition centuries old;
We live up to that in the S.C. fleet,
When on convoy and patrol.

Our purpose is like the Concord Light,
A continuous vigil at sea;
Protecting ships from submarines,
To keep our country free.

Preface

December 7, 1941. "A date which will live in infamy." What a significant milestone for those of us then living, for it changed our lives forever and altered our plans drastically! A quiet, peaceful Sunday afternoon in the States — clear and cold in the Northeastern and upper Midwestern areas, a last episode of Indian summer in the Southern and Southwestern regions. We who experienced that day vividly remember where we were and what we were doing when we heard of the attack on Pearl Harbor. Don W. Terry, a 1938 graduate of McMurry College, teacher as well as band director at the High School in Plains, Texas, was painting a desk he had bought the previous day. George A. Burrell, thirty years of age, graduate of Columbia University and Brooklyn Law School, with a fledgling law practice in Brooklyn, was driving back to New York City after a weekend of skiing in Vermont. Ronald B. Balcom, age thirty-two, whose education included St. Paul's Prep School, Lafayette University and the School of Business at New York University, engaged in business in Richmond, Virginia, had just completed the Sunday buffet at the Commonwealth Club. James T. Moore, twenty-one years old, working seven days a week on the swing shift at the Lynchburg Foundry in Virginia, was awakened by friends with the news. James B. Hannah, twenty years old, from Minneapolis and a senior at Harvard, heard the news on the radio and promptly shouted it out to fellow students from the top of the staircase in the Leverett House library. Your author, twenty years old, from Sweetwater, Texas, senior at Amherst College, had just settled down in a reading room at the college library to prepare for Monday's classes, when a fraternity brother came in and excitedly said, "The Japs are bombing Pearl Harbor!" It seemed so preposterous to me; I thought he must be kidding. Along with a couple of other students we went outside to my 1941 Chevrolet convertible, which had a radio. Then, in disbelief, we heard an announcer in Pearl Harbor reporting the events taking place before his very eyes. We could hear the roar of the attacking airplanes, and the explosions of bombs hitting their targets. It was an eerie feeling to hear the attacks as they were being described by the radio announcer. The only similar situation I have experienced since was to hear *and* see the live CNN broadcast from Bagdad the night the Persian Gulf War began.

After listening to the radio broadcast, we drove to the fraternity house where the matter was being discussed excitedly. Later, students and faculty gathered together in Johnson Chapel at the college where President Stanley King and several faculty members spoke to us about what likely lay ahead.

Little did I realize that crisp, clear, quiet Sunday in New England that in only thirteen months I would be reporting on board the USS *SC-761* at Miami. Or that the men named above, as well as others from such places as Star City, Arkansas; Dunkirk, New York; Franklin, New Hampshire; Turnbridge, North Dakota; Cameron, Texas, and countless other diverse places would do likewise. We all had a rendezvous with the *SC-761,* and strangers once, our lives would become entwined while, on that subchaser, we participated in naval activities in the South Pacific.

All classes at Amherst College were canceled for Monday, and we listened intently as President Roosevelt addressed a joint session of Congress and requested a joint declaration of war against Japan. Roosevelt, like Winston Churchill, had a masterful command of the English language, and he galvanized the fighting resolve of the nation in that spellbinding speech. It was a somber occasion, full of high drama, and through radio the nation heard the voting by Congress. Jeanette Rankin of Montana, the lone female member of Congress, with a frail and anguished voice cast the only nay vote. At this time there were no negative votes among the general public. A nation that had been so terribly divided concerning the war which had raged in Europe since 1939 (exemplified by Congress having extended the one-year draft by only one vote as late as September 1941) was now absolutely, firmly committed to avenge Pearl Harbor. Henceforth, nothing would be the same. Now, whatever plans we once had would be irrevocably altered. Jim Hannah would not be going to Harvard Law School the next fall. Jim Moore would quit his defense job at the Lynchburg Foundry to enlist in the navy. I would cancel my acceptance to Harvard Business School.

War changed everything from the lives of people to the products of industry. How best to serve your country was uppermost on the minds of everyone. The young and able-bodied, male and female, would serve in the military; the others would serve in war plants or in countless volunteer efforts. Recruiting stations around the country were swamped. Officer teams visited the college campuses pitching various officer candidate programs. Like most of my classmates at Amherst, I joined the navy's V-7 program, enlisting as an apprentice seaman on 1 April 1942 at Springfield, Massachusetts. Jim Hannah did likewise at Harvard. Ronald Balcom, with significant sailing and business experience, received a direct commission as a lieutenant, junior grade. Unbeknownst to us at the time, we would end up serving together on the USS *SC-761*, sailing the ship to the South Pacific and engaging in some of the Solomon Islands campaigns among other naval activities.

This is the story of the *SC-761*, a very small ship in a very big war. Since I, personally, only experienced thirteen months of that story, the rest has been pieced together by me through interviews of former members of ship's company from coast- to-coast, along with research of official records. That subchaser and its crew had a distinct part to play in the Pacific theatre during WWII, and that part was handled with such skill that on one memorable occasion in the Solomons the *SC-761* and its crew were commended personally by their task force commander, Rear Adm. T. S. Wilkinson. The *SC-761* was manned mainly by reservists, many of whom had never seen salt water prior to their naval service. Yet these men performed their duties in the best of naval traditions. It was an example of the civilian navy at its best. It is with high regard and deep respect for the men who served on this ship that I have undertaken this project.

— J. HENRY DOSCHER, JR.

CHAPTER 1

In the Beginning

Fortunately, several shipyards devoted to the building of wooden ships, principally yachting sailboats, existed in the United States when war broke out in Europe in 1939. Many such shipyards were located in New England. Among these was one known as W. A. Robinson, Inc.

William A Robinson, adventurer and author of *10,000 Leagues Over The Sea*, came to Ipswich, Massachusetts, in 1936 following his solo trip around the world in a thirty-foot sloop. He married Florence Crane, whose family had a summer home and other property at Ipswich. His dream was to build fine sailing yachts; so with funds supplied by his wife, Robinson and marine historian Howard I. Chapelle built a shipyard in the little bay where Fox Creek enters the Ipswich River.

Wooden ships had been built in the area around nearby Essex since before the American revolution, but their heyday was long since past. With America still struggling from the Great Depression and its aftermath, many such shipyards had closed or were in serious decline. Accordingly, there was an available work force of experienced shipbuilders skilled in all phases of constructing wooden crafts, including use of the adze and broadadze—ancient tools of the shipbuilder. These were men whose fathers and grandfathers and even great-grandfathers had built such ships.

The Robinson shipyard began in a modest way, constructing its first vessel, the seventy-foot Baltimore clipper "Swift," in 1937. Robinson and his partner, Chapelle, soon parted ways; fortunately Robinson continued his little shipyard, and it was still in existence when World War II came on the scene. With the rise of the dictators in Europe, the navy recognized early that if the United States be-

1

came involved in a war, there would be a significant need for small antisubmarine craft constructed in minimum time. As early as 1937, the navy held design competitions from which were selected a modern adaption of the old subchaser designs from World War I. Based on this new design, a few subchasers were built, tested, and placed in commission in 1941 prior to Pearl Harbor.

With the declaration of war upon Japan, shipbuilding became urgent. The German submarine menace necessitated a large force of ships capable of antisubmarine warfare. Generally a subchaser, the hull of which is crafted of seasoned wood, can be built in the relatively short time of about five months. As a result, the navy turned to all shipyards that had been building any type of wooden craft in order to quickly obtain subchasers to meet the critical need for escort type ships. Immediately others sprang up—some experienced and some not.

Like other shipyards, Robinson went to war. Its first contract was for two subchasers, *SC-676* and *SC-677*, with keels laid in January and February 1942. Receiving a second navy contract in late February, the Robinson shipyard began to expand both its number of ways which to build ships as well as its work force. Experienced shipbuilders from all over Essex County and southern New Hampshire were called out of retirement, some in their seventies, one in his eighties. They were highly skilled craftsmen and shipwrights, and their products became outstanding examples of their significant abilities.

The *SC-761* was a product of their craftsmanship. On 14 March 1942 the keels for it and its sister ship, the *SC-760*, with which it would cross paths many times in the future, were each laid on two new ways of the Robinson shipyard. Both ships had an actual length of 110 feet, ten inches, with a beam of eighteen feet. Each had a draft of five feet, five inches, and displaced 116 tons. Twin screws powered by two 500-horsepower diesel engines produced a top speed of slightly more than 15 knots.

They had the lines of a fine yacht. A high bow and a sweeping deckline sloping to a broad stern gave these ships a rakish appearance. The pilot house, which also housed the chart room, ASW, and subsequent radar equipment, was located about one-third of the way abaft the bow. A flying bridge was above the pilot house. The quarterdeck extended from the aft end of the pilot house to the amidships area. All other facilities were below deck.

These ships had facilities for a maximum crew of twenty-seven men and three officers. There were forward and aft crew quarters.

The forward crew quarters contained more bunks and lockers, while the aft crew quarters also served as the mess hall with the ajoining galley just forward. The radio shack and ship's office were below the forward one-third portion of the pilot house, while the officers' quarters were below the balance of the pilot house.

Immediately aft of the officers' quarters was the engine room. Fuel tanks were in between the galley and the engine room. The ship's water tanks were located between the forward crew quarters and the radio shack/ship's office areas. Below the fantail was a large lazaret — the only storeroom of any consequence. Therefore, officers and crew lived and operated in extremely compact quarters.

These ships were well-conceived for their designed duty. The initial armament consisted of a 3-inch/23 gun mounted forward, a port and starboard 20MM gun on each side of the quarterdeck, and two depth charge racks with two K-gun projectors on the fantail. Appropriate ammunition was stored in ready boxes on the deck near the guns. Twin rocket launchers, known as mousetraps, were located on the bow just forward of the 3-inch/23 gun.

Final acceptance trials having occurred on 22 September, the *SC-761* was now ready to be commissioned and accepted into the fleet. Early on the morning of 24 September, the remaining fourteen members of the precommissioning detail which had been assembled at the Receiving Station of the Boston Navy Yard arrived in Ipswich by commuter train. These men joined the six petty officers and Lt. (jg) F. D. Andrus, the initial commanding officer, and Ens. A. W. McGuire, the initial executive officer, all of whom had been in Ipswich since mid-August during the final construction phase and basic fitting-out of the *SC-761*.

All hands reported on board before noon, stowed their gear, and prepared for the commissioning ceremony of the ship and its final acceptance by the navy. Among those preparations, the executive officer had drawn up the watch, quarter and station bill, detailing the assignments of the crew for all drills and special details. Dockside, on a beautiful New England fall afternoon, under bright sunshine with broken clouds and a mild temperature of 74 degrees, all was ready as navy officials came aboard. In a brief, but formal, ceremony at 1445 prompt with the crew at attention on the quarterdeck the orders whereby the navy accepted and commissioned the ship were read. In turn, Lieutenant Andrus read his orders detailing him as commanding officer. With the national ensign hoisted aft, the Union Jack at the bow, and the commission pennant raised to the truck on the mast, the initial watch section was posted to duty. The

SC-761 was now part of the navy but not yet ready for fleet duty, as this was only the beginning. The rest of the day was spent taking on stores and topping off the fuel and water tanks.

Having cast off all lines and with one long blast on the whistle, the *SC-761* pulled smartly away from the builder's dock at 1320 the next day at high tide. Standing down the Ipswich River and into the Atlantic, the ship was under way to the Boston Navy Yard for fitting-out and later for shakedown. While it was only a three-hour trip under bright sunshine, a calm sea gave this rather green crew a chance to get its sea legs. By 1647, they tied up at Commonwealth Pier 1 alongside the *SC-760* which had been commissioned some ten days earlier.

The next day they were under way to calibrate the compass and run the degaussing range. When they returned to Pier 1, it was discovered that a bearing on the main shaft had burned out, the first of several equipment problems. Repairs delayed the final fitting-out by two days. The fitting-out and initial part of shakedown took approximately two weeks at Boston and at Provincetown. This was followed by additional fitting-out and shakedown procedures at New London, Connecticut, and at Tompkinsville, Staten Island, New York. Due to engine problems and one steering failure, some six weeks were involved.

On 7 November, during one of its visits to New London, an enemy submarine was reported in the eastern areas of Long Island Sound. Promptly, the *SC-761* and other subchasers joined the USS *Champlain* in an antisubmarine search. Operating in its assigned sector, the *SC-761* developed a submarine contact with its ASW gear. With Lieutenant Andrus at the conn, it made a run for the sub and dropped four depth charges. Only a large oil slick came to the surface. No other evidence was ever found; no kill was confirmed. Nevertheless, this inexperienced but cocky crew maintained that it had a kill, and just as gunfighters of the Old West had notched their pistols, they painted a sinking submarine on both sides of the pilot house along with one hash mark.

No greater morale booster could have occurred. With enthusiasm the crew of the *SC-761* was ready for whatever duty lay ahead.

CHAPTER 2

Tompkinsville and Miami

Having completed its trials on 2 December 1942, the *SC-761* reported to ComEastSeaFron for duty. It was assigned to Tompkinsville on Staten Island in New York harbor. The SC-761 was now part of the fleet. Other subchasers, including its sister ship, were located at Tompkinsville. The *SC-761* began convoy duty between New York harbor and the Cape May, New Jersey area. While some ships were escorted south, generally the subchasers sailed to Cape May where they picked up freighters coming out of the Delaware River. Each convoy formed and proceeded along the New Jersey coast to New York, where the freighters later became part of a larger convoy to cross the North Atlantic.

After one such round-trip to Cape May, Ensign McGuire, the initial executive officer, apparently a victim of chronic seasickness, was detached. Ens. H. L. Quinn reported as his replacement. Later, in January, when the ship would come to Miami, I would relieve Ensign Quinn as executive officer. Fortunately, two former members of ship's company, one of whom was a plank owner, furnished me detailed accounts of activities prior to my arrival. Their reports amplified and confirmed matters in the official records.

The voyages from Tompkinsville to Cape May and back generally took two full days, sometimes three, depending on the particular convoy. George A. Burrell, then QM2c, who had reported aboard in October to relieve the original quartermaster, had considerable experience sailing yachts before the war. He had made prior yachting trips from New York to Florida and was quite familiar with the East Coast area. He reports that on one convoy trip from Cape May to New York two merchant ships ran aground on Five Fathom shoal in spite of warnings he and his skipper had relayed to the convoy commander stationed in one of the five merchant ships.

5

In Burrell's opinion, the convoy commander was ordering a turn to the north too soon and ships on the port side of the convoy might go aground. Unfortunately, the convoy commander ignored this warning. The Five Fathom lightship clearly marked that shoal which must be well cleared to seaward prior to turning north. The log of the *SC-761* reflects this incident, stating that two of the merchant ships, one British the other Brazilian, soon ran aground. The *SC-761* was left behind to screen these two ships while navy tugs worked to free them from this shoal. Thus, this was a longer trip than subchasers normally experienced on such a run.

The weather in December was cold and miserable. The gear on the topsides of the subchasers often became covered with ice. Men needed special protective gear to guard against frostbite. Lookouts had to be rotated frequently. Great quantities of hot coffee were consumed on each watch. Fortunately, the ship had about two or three days in Tompkinsville between each convoy trip, which enabled the crew to recover from arduous conditions endured on a ship with limited quarters. Christmas Eve and Christmas Day were spent in New York harbor; New Year's Eve was spent at sea.

In the meantime, a significant need had arisen in the South Pacific Fleet for antisubmarine ships to provide convoy escort duty. The available destroyers were needed for combat duty, and destroyer escorts were not yet available due to lengthly construction times. Under the circumstances by Cominch order 051435 of January 1943 this ship and its sister ship were transferred to the South Pacific Force. Both ships were directed to proceed to Panama and report to ComPaSeaFron for onward routing prior to 10 February. In the interim, they were directed to proceed together as soon as possible to Miami and report to ComGulfSeaFron to be equipped for distant service and onward routing. As a result, the *SC-761* and *SC-760* got under way for Miami on 11 January.

Miami was the home of the Submarine Chaser Training Center, known in the navy as SCTC. It was headed by Captain McDaniel, a salty veteran of antisubmarine warfare. He had organized this school at Pier 2 on Biscayne Bay. The classrooms had been partitioned out of the warehouses on the pier. Initially, every officer and man assigned to subchasers went through this training center for an eight-week crash course. The instructors were experienced navy chiefs and officers. The instruction was all practical, no theory. Each student was taught how to do something such as celestial navigation, without explanation as to why such procedure was used. This was much different from the astronomy course I had taken at Amherst College, which included navigation, or from the more leisurely pace at which navigation had been taught in the ninety-day course conducted by the midshipman school at Northwestern University. Needless to say, the background of that earlier college course considerably helped my grade in both the navigation courses at SCTC and at midshipman school.

Jim Hannah and I had gone through the naval indoctrination course at Notre Dame and the midshipman school at Northwestern. We knew of each other, but since Doscher and Hannah are so far apart in the alphabet, we were never in the same company nor billeted on the same deck at Tower Hall. But we ended up together on the *SC-761*, and that would begin what has become a lifelong friendship.

When ordered to SCTC at Miami for further training, we thought we might have time to relax in the sun. Nothing was farther from the truth. The instruction at SCTC was six and one-half days per week. Only Sunday afternoons were free. We did get vacation on Christmas Day, and as a result Jim married Rosemary, his sweetheart from Minneapolis, on Christmas Eve. She came to Miami with their parents for the wedding at the little Episcopal church located only a short distance from the school.

The practical instruction and training we received at SCTC gave us our first experience in shiphandling as well as the functions of all personnel on board a subchaser. Being capably force-fed the myriad information needed for operating subchasers, we were at least given a reasonable chance to succeed. The enlisted men received a modified course of instruction, related principally to the duties of their ratings. It was necessary for all to receive training in gunnery.

Our course at SCTC was in its last week when the *SC-761* arrived in Miami and tied up to berth "A" at Pier 2 early the morning of 15 January. Ammunition was immediately unloaded. At 1706 the ship proceeded to the Merrill-Stevens Shipyard near Pier 2 and tied up alongside the *SC-760*. The next morning shipyard work began in order to ready the ship for duty in the South Pacific. Much had to be accomplished in a short time, so workmen were everywhere about the ship. The 3-inch/23 gun was immediately removed. A new 40MM gun was installed in the bow area where the former 3-inch/23 gun had been located. It was a dual-purpose gun that could fire either antiaircraft (AA) shells or armor-piercing (AP) shells.

New ammunition ready-boxes were installed that could handle both types of this ammunition. An additional 20MM gun was installed on a new circular platform constructed over the galley area, with its aft end just forward of the hatch leading down to the aft crew quarters. This necessitated the installation of another 20MM ammunition ready-box on the deck nearby. These new guns were critically necessary since Japanese aircraft would be our most significant threat in the South Pacific. This threat had not been a concern for a ship originally outfitted for convoy patrol along the Atlantic seaboard. Radar, which was now available, was installed. The basic radar equipment and controls were installed within the pilot house on its port side. The radar antenna and housing were installed at the masthead, which was specially braced to accommodate such new equipment. Since the ship would be operating in tropical areas near the equator, ventilation — not ice — was a major concern. Accordingly, very extensive blower systems were installed to alleviate problems of extreme heat. The ship was then placed on blocks, and the workmen cleaned and painted the bottom.

After the *SC-761* entered the shipyard, SCTC began a grand reshuffling of personnel on the ship. On 16 January I was called to Operations and given orders to report the next day to the USS *SC-761* as its executive officer. This would give me time to pack up my gear and check out of the nearby Albert Motel. I called home to tell my widowed mother, alone at the time, that I would be going to sea but I knew not where or when. The ship was in the shipyard, so it would be a few days before it sailed. Since I was her only son, Mother surprised me in a few days by making the long train trip from Sweetwater, Texas, to Miami.

As ordered, I reported on board the *SC-761* at 0800 the next day, and relieved Ensign Quinn as executive officer. The commanding officer, Lieutenant Andrus, told me he expected to be relieved any day. Two days later, on 19 January, Lt. (jg) Ronald B. Balcom, reported on board and relieved Mr. Andrus. That same day, Ens. James B. Hannah reported for duty as third officer. The commanding officer also assumed the duties as morale officer and ASW officer. As executive officer, I was assigned the additional duties of navigator, personnel officer, administrative officer, and gunnery officer. Jim Hannah became the engineering officer, supply officer, communications officer, medical officer, and recreation/welfare officer. Also, he was to carry out the functions that would come under the purview of a first lieutenant on a larger ship. We decided to subsist in the general mess with the crew, so no wardroom mess treasurer was necessary.

At this time, six senior experienced petty officers were transferred from the ship, and newly trained men were sent to replace them. The ship received a radarman for the first time, as well as additional newly trained seamen. At last the *SC-761* had its designated quota of three officers and twenty-four men.

On 24 January, the work completed, the ship left the yard and moored alongside Pier 3 at SCTC. On 24 January we conducted a dock trial of the main engines. We then got under way for engine trials at sea and to test-fire the new 40MM and the new 20MM guns. The crew, many of whom were new to the ship, was also exercised at general quarters and given test drills.

The commanding officer reported that the ship was ready for sea. Those of us on board had no idea when we would begin our long journey to the South Pacific. The waiting began but we at least had a few more days of liberty in Miami.

Among the officers, we let Jim Hannah have each night ashore, since he was on his honeymoon. Two-thirds of the crew had liberty each evening, and most of the young men had girlfriends in Miami. In fact, at this time Don Terry met Margaret, the young lady who later became his wife. Those last few days in the States were important to us, and we savored each minute to its fullest. We knew not what we might encounter in the unknown duties that lay ahead. We knew not when or whether we would return stateside.

Our destiny was in the hands of others.

CHAPTER 3

Miami to Balboa

None of us on any ship knew exactly when these subchasers would depart Miami, only that departure was imminent. The liberty sections of the *SC-761* reported aboard ship each morning by 0700. Quarters were at 0800. Their girlfriends, wives, or other relatives knew that if their particular crewman did not come ashore in the evening, chances were his ship had been put to sea. The naval station maintained very tight security; no dependent or friend was ever allowed on the premises of SCTC or the piers where the subchasers were moored. However, the piers and the subchasers were clearly visible from a nearby bridge across Biscayne Bay which linked Miami and Miami Beach. Twice during a day Jim Hannah's wife, Rosemary, left the Albert Motel and walked out to the bridge to see if *SC-761* was still moored at a pier. When she went to her observation point in mid-afternoon of 4 February, the subchasers at Pier 3 were gone! Slowly she made her way back to the motel, sobbing. Her honeymoon had encountered a sudden hiatus, the extent of which was so painfully uncertain. She told my mother, who was staying at the nearby Venetian Hotel, that the ships had gone. As a result, they went back to Minneapolis and Sweetwater, respectively. Now they could only wait and hope.

For us on the *SC-761* the departure was just as sudden and just as dramatic. Each commanding officer of the nine subchasers moored at Pier 3 was called to operations at 0830 that morning, with the word passed to top off with fuel and water and to take on any last minute provisions. Our skipper returned at 1000 and advised the crew that we were headed for Panama. At noon the subchasers began to pull away from the pier, one by one. Standing down the channel, the line of ships headed for the open sea. Except for the two engineers on duty in the engine room, all hands went topside to have a last look at Miami. Hearing a bark, I was surprised to see a small, shaggy dog on the forecastle. Upon inquiry, I discovered that Galford, newly promoted to chief boatswain's mate, had brought the dog aboard during the night before we sailed. He firmly maintained that the dog "just followed me back to the ship." The crew immediately adopted the dog as our mascot. After considerable discussion among the crew, the dog was dubbed "Feathers." In the navy, reservists were often called feather merchants, and since some eighty percent of the crew and all three officers were reservists, the crew decided Feathers was an appropriate name. We now had another member of ship's company.

Clearing the entrance buoy, the nine subchasers continued in column formation, increasing speed to 13 knots. They hugged the coastline so that the Gulf Stream would have minimum effect on their speed. In the lead was the *SC-641*, followed in order by the *SCs 699, 982, 761, 760, 518, 981, 698,* and *648*. Assisted by Quartermaster Burrell, I was busy with navigation, and our closeness to shore combined with the existence of numerous lighthouses enabled me to have actual practice with piloting. The lighthouses are very accurately located on the charts. By taking bearings of a lighthouse when it is broad on the bow (045 degrees) and when it later is abeam (090 degrees) the ship and knowing the actual speed and the elapsed time interval between those two sightings, one is able to plot the exact distance of the ship from the lighthouse when it is abeam. By this procedure, a navigator is merely making use of an isosceles triangle to determine the position of the ship when abeam a specific lighthouse.

As navigator, I was up and down all night with the quartermaster taking those bearings on various lighthouses and plotting our positions. First was Cayspoint Light abeam to starboard at 2050. Then Molasses Light at 2235. On 5 February Alligator Light, near Islamorda, was checked off at 0015 on the mid-watch, followed by Tennessee Light at 0235. The passing of each light caused the formation to make slight course changes as we sailed down the Florida Keys. At 0517 American Shoal Light, near Key West, was abeam to starboard, followed by Sand Key Light at 0727.

We were making good time as we sailed through the Florida Straits. Having our last glimpse of the States, we headed into the easternmost portion of the Gulf of Mexico, preparing to sail around the western edge of Cuba. That evening at 2115 Punta Gobernadora Light, just east of Havana, was abeam to port. On 6 February at

0110 during the mid-watch came Cayo Justias Light abeam to port causing a course change to 235 degrees true. At 0900 San Antonio Light on the extreme western edge of Cuba was bearing 130 degrees true, distance eight miles. Forty-five minutes later course was changed to 128 degrees true, resulting in San Antonio Light coming abeam to port at 1050. Soon we would be leaving the outer reaches of the Gulf of Mexico and entering the Caribbean Sea. On 7 February Grand Cayman was abeam to port at 1155. By 1345 course was changed to 170 degrees true, and we were on the final leg to Panama.

Each day the crew exercised and participated in drills at general quarters since there were so many new members of the crew as well as three new officers. Everyone was becoming acquainted with his job, his station and his function at each drill, as well as learning more about each other. It was a time for confidence building. The weather and sea cooperated beautifully except in the Florida Straits. While many of the crew developed a queasy feeling, only one became truly seasick. Brandel, a very young fireman, first class, who had never seen salt water before he joined the crew at Miami, developed a chronic case of seasickness. Shortly after the ship left the entrance buoy at Miami he was heaving over the railing. By the time we had passed through the Florida Straits, he was spitting up blood. Needless to say, he was replaced by another fireman while we were in Panama. I might mention that once we reached Panama, Brandel literally crawled out onto the dock and kissed the ground. Never was terra firma more welcomed by anyone.

Otherwise all was going smoothly — too smoothly it seemed — until during the mid-watch on 8 February at 0120, the *SC-761* completely lost steering control. This is a serious problem especially since the ships were zigzagging on the trip to Panama in a darkened ship condition. Jim Hannah was the officer of the deck, while Moore, then a seaman, second class, and a new member of the crew, was standing his first wheel watch at night. Moore vividly recalls the incident and the helpless feeling as the ship would not respond to any movement of the helm. Through the voice tube to the flying bridge he cried out the problem to Ensign Hannah. Hannah immediately, but briefly, broke radio silence to warn the following subchasers to stand clear and called the commanding officer to the bridge. The rest of the ships slowed to 6 knots, while the *SC-761* attempted repairs. Two other engineers were aroused, the lazarette was opened, and the engineers entered that compartment to ascertain the problem. A steering cable had come loose.

Working in poor light, struggling against time, N. A. Singer, Jr.,

MoMM2c, from St. Louis, and part of the precommissioning detail, corrected the problem. Fortunately, he had been aboard earlier when a similar steering failure had occurred in New York Harbor, and thus knew how to go about reconnecting the steering cable. With everything back in working order, speed was increased to 15 knots, and shortly before daylight the *SC-761* rejoined the formation, falling in at the stern. The group resumed formation speed of 12 knots. We had come through our first problem with flying colors. We had been tested, and we passed.

The following day, 9 February, at 1245 the lookout cried "land ahoy." Panama was in sight. Two hours later we were at the approaches to Colon Harbor channel and speed was slowed to 8 knots. At 1515 we passed the Colon Harbor entrance buoy abeam to starboard, and speed was changed to 6 knots. By blinker light we were given our respective berthing assignments. At 1715 we had moored port side to Pier 2, Berth Baker, of the submarine base in the area known as Coco Solo. Immediately forward of us at the pier was the *SC-730*, captained by Lt. Robinson McIlvaine, who was an old friend of our skipper. Because Merrill-Stevens in Miami had been swamped with work at the time the *SC-730* had come to Panama three weeks earlier to have its shipyard modifications accomplished. The *SC-641*, whose skipper was Lt. (jg) Robert E. Lee Taylor, and which had led us to Panama, tied up alongside the *SC-730*. Thus began a long relationship between these three subchasers, whose skippers had been friends in New York City before the war.

Liberty until midnight for two-thirds of the crew was promptly announced. Our skipper elected to stay aboard this first evening, so Jim Hannah and I decided to take in the town. We had no knowledge of the uniform of the day for officers in Panama. The captain of our midshipman school at Northwestern had given us lengthy lectures about being "an officer and a gentleman," as well as about all manner of naval etiquette. Jim and I decided we could not go wrong by wearing dress whites, which had been the uniform for our Sunday afternoon off duty in Miami. Dressed accordingly, we went ashore, caught a taxi (old Ford Model A touring car), and went into Colon. We were the only officers in dress whites in town! We discovered the uniform was khaki with short sleeves, open collar and knee length trousers. We stood out like a sore thumb!

In each bar there were young females, known as "Blue Mooners" or "B Girls," who would sit down and talk with you if you bought them a drink. They always ordered a drink called a Blue Moon, which was flavored iced tea. Unbeknownst to us at the time, at one dollar it was the most expensive drink available. All other drinks in those days were only twenty-five cents.

As we entered each bar, we were swamped by B Girls. Our white uniforms and twenty-one-year-old baby faces said that we were the new guys in town. As such, we would not know how expensive those drinks could be for only a few minutes of chit-chat. After several young girls sat at our table and each ordered three drinks in about fifteen minutes, we were presented with the check. It was then we learned we had been taken to the cleaners. Thus, we disdained any of these conversations when we sampled other bars in town. Definitely thereafter our uniform was khaki.

Before Jim Hannah and I returned to the ship we stumbled upon Panama Hatties, a bar with a floor show. It featured Jade, a young female dancer reputed to be half-girl and half-ape. With the band providing a wild Latin beat reminiscent of the "Bolero," she gave a rather sensuous performance. While it most definitely lacked the sophistication of the "Folies Bergere," which I had seen in Paris as a prep school senior, her act catered to the same basic instincts. Jade at Panama Hatties became an outstanding attraction, well known to any of the fleet that transited the canal. Because of her popularity, she was later featured in *Life Magazine*.

While we waited for the authorities to schedule our transit of the canal, we enjoyed five nights at Coco Solo. We could not transit the canal immediately because facilities at Balboa, on the Pacific side, were crowded. Furthermore, our convoy was not scheduled to depart Balboa until 18 February. On Friday evening, 12 February, the officers of the subchasers had a farewell cocktail and dinner party at the Washington Hotel in Colon. I had duty that evening, so Ronald Balcom and Jim Hannah represented the *SC-761*. It was a memorable occasion, full of camaraderie worthy of a swashbuckling Hollywood movie. Errol Flynn would have felt very much at home if he had been present that evening.

The first subchasers transited the canal on 13 February, a day after the tanker USS *Pecos*. We followed on Sunday, 14 February. The *SC-761* cast off its lines in the early morning at 0725 and was under way. Four subchasers entered a lock at one time. For safety reasons, each ship was towed through each lock by electric locomotives, known as mules. At 1120 we entered the Gatun Locks, and once having cleared them we sailed into Gatun Lake. This is a large, twenty-two-mile long fresh-water lake, and fresh water is ideal for cleaning a ship. Chief Galford, who as an apprentice seaman had served on a battleship with teakwood decking, had his deck crew turn to as he taught them the joys of "holy stoning" a wooden deck. The deck was wet down and fine sand spread upon it; the deck crew rubbed the sand on the deck with firebrick. It was a back-breaking job but it produced a beautiful deck. As far as I have been able to discover, the *SC-761* may have been the only subchaser that "holy stoned" a deck during WWII. To this day, Moore and the other seamen indelibly recall this experience.

From Gatun Lake we proceeded over the Continental Divide into and through the majestic Gaillard Cut. By 1730 that same day, we had entered Pedro Miguel Locks, and at 1855 the Miraflores Locks by which we were lowered into the salt water of Balboa Harbor on the Pacific side of Panama. In all, it had been a fifty-one-mile journey, fascinating to each of us. We were awestruck by the sheer magnitude of this engineering marvel, especially in view of the fact that ships must be raised and lowered approximately eighty-five feet during a transit of the canal. After clearing Miraflores Locks, we proceeded to Pier 18 in Balboa Harbor and moored alongside the *SC-730* which had made its transit the day before.

The serious portion of the adventure for the *SC-761* was soon to begin.

CHAPTER 4

Balboa to Bora Bora

On 16 February, the last of the subchasers which would proceed at this time to the South Pacific completed their transit of the canal and arrived alongside the piers in Balboa. There was a feverish last-minute scramble to take on supplies and equipment. Quartermasters requisitioned the charts needed for the Pacific Ocean areas and turned in most charts for the Atlantic. Large quantities of food were obtained for use en route to Bora Bora, the longest leg of the trip which lay ahead of us. On the *SC-761* the cook filled the galley ice boxes with eggs and fresh bread, the most critical fresh food items.

On 17 February the skippers of each ship in the convoy had a detailed briefing and conference aboard the "mother ship" of the convoy, the USS *Pecos*, a navy tanker. During the preceding ten days, the skipper of the *SC-730*, Lt. Robinson McIlvaine, had engaged in detailed conferences with the skipper and other personnel of the *Pecos* concerning convoy matters. This included refueling and repairs at sea, and related matters. In fact, the *Pecos* would be carrying as temporary personnel various men with expert ratings to handle all types of repairs that might occur en route. All such matters were covered thoroughly for all commanding officers at these detailed briefings. Everything was in readiness for departure pursuant to ComPaSeaFron despatch 171849 of February.

At 0830 on 18 February, the subchasers, led by the *SC-730*, began to pull away from the piers. They proceeded out into the Gulf of Panama to provide an antisubmarine screen for the other ships in the convoy. It was a perfect day with clear skies, bright sunshine and almost no wind. The calm sea was most welcome, as we looked into the beautiful blue waters for which the Pacific Ocean is renowned. Following behind the *SC-730* were the tanker *Pecos*, five mine-

16

sweepers (YMSs), sixteen landing craft (LCIs), one seagoing fleet tug (AT), and the net tender (YN).

In short order the convoy formed around the *Pecos,* in which was located the convoy commander, P. N. Gunnell. Positioned immediately astern of the *Pecos,* on one of its quarters, was the fleet tug; on the other quarter was the net tender. The sixteen LCIs were grouped in four columns of four each, aft of the fleet tug and the net tender. The five YMSs were arranged in a semicircle. One was directly forward of the *Pecos,* one abeam to port, and one broad on the port bow of the *Pecos,* with a similiar arrangement to starboard of the *Pecos.* The eleven subchasers formed a circular screen around the entire convoy. The escort commander was Lt. Robinson McIlvaine in the *SC-730* and that ship took the lead screen position directly forward of the *Pecos.* The *SC-761* was abeam to port of the convoy.

The subchasers which formed this escort differed slightly from the group that had departed from Miami together. A couple of our original group were held back for a later convoy, and several new ones joined us in Panama. Thus the escort for this convoy was composed of the *SCs 730, 518, 641, 648, 698, 701, 739, 751, 760, 761,* and *982.*

As the convoy headed out of the Gulf of Panama and into the broad expanse of the Pacific Ocean, it passed San Jose Island to port. This would be our last glimpse of the continent for months to come. We were now en route to Bora Bora in the French Society Islands. Our course of travel was along the equator for much of the way. In respect to the weather and the sea, we were very fortunate. We encountered no truly rough weather; an occasional heavy, rolling sea was the most we experienced. We began a slow, often monotonous routine. The LCIs limited the convoy speed to 10 knots. The convoy zigzagged as it made its way, in darkened ship conditions of course, and this kept the watch sections on their toes at all times. We all had to be especially careful regarding the LCIs. They each had a newfangled electric steering system which could cause any one of them to suddenly make almost a ninety-degree turn. Happily, such an unexpected maneuver never occurred.

While a subchaser can carry enough fuel to cruise about ten days, the convoy routine called for refueling at sea every three or four days, just in case the *Pecos* was lost due to a submarine attack. Furthermore, subchasers do not have any equipment which would enable them to convert salt water to fresh water. Thus the amount of fresh water a subchaser's tanks will hold is a very limiting factor unless the fresh water is strictly conserved. The YMSs had similar limiting factors. The *Pecos* could supply all the diesel fuel we needed, but only limited quantities of fresh water were available. Accordingly, each third or fourth day, the SCs and the YMSs took on fuel, limited amouts of fresh water, and some provisions from the *Pecos*. This gave the officers and crews of the SCs and YMSs significant experience with the refueling procedures at sea. After a few of those operations, it became possible for a ship to complete refueling in less than three-quarters of an hour.

Because the available amount of fresh water was so critical, the showers in the crew's quarters were closed. The engineers on the *SC-761* rigged up a saltwater shower on the main deck, amidships, near the hatch to the engine room. Special soap for salt water was available. The men used the deck shower generally at dusk. Since our course followed along the equator and its adjoining areas during most of this portion of our trip, we often encountered heavy tropical showers in the afternoons. Those members of the crew not on duty would don their bathing suits and clean themselves as best they could with the rainwater. Some caught rainwater in buckets so as to rinse off the salt from the saltwater shower.

This portion of our journey gave me extremely practical experience in celestial navigation. Each day all subchasers reported to the convoy commander their 0800 positions by simultaneous flag-hoist at 0810. Thus, we could correllate our positions. Being our navigator, I was up each morning well before sunrise to take starsights with the sextant. The quartermaster assisted me by recording the readings as I called them off. He also recorded the time on a stop watch we used with the ship's chronometer. This was done with the greatest accuracy in order to precisely determine the ship's exact position on earth, based upon the position of various known stars in the heavens. In fact, the ship's chronometer was checked for accuracy once each day by radio time signals from the Naval Observatory in Washington, D.C.

I was forever grateful to that army of unemployed mathematicians engaged by the WPA during the depths of the depression to calculate (in the days before computers) various figures one could use to minimize the time involved in converting the starsight angles to meaningful data. The resulting H.O. 214 and related volumes were in the chart rooms of every navy ship. This saved navigators the laborious and detailed calculations necessary when using the former Bowditch procedure I had learned in an astronomy course at Amherst College. Furthermore, the chance of error in one's calculations was greatly diminished. In addition to the morning and evening starsights, I used the sun to determine latitude (LAN) each noontime.

On one segment of this trip, we had to improvise a chart. The quartermaster had failed to obtain a chart of one portion of the open ocean. We just used the back of another chart that contained the correct latitudes, drew in the latitude and longitude lines, and numbered them. Knowing there were no reefs or islands in this open expanse of the Pacific, we felt comfortable doing this. Thus for a small segment of this trip, our chart was a blank white sheet with latitude and longitude lines drawn in by pencil. As a result we could still report our 0800 positions as well as plot our positions each day to the convoy commander.

The crew had little in the way of entertainment other than a few decks of cards, cribbage, the radio, and the record player. No movie facilities were available on the subchasers, but the ship had obtained a fine record player in Miami, which the radiomen installed in the radio shack. This sound system carried music from AM and short-wave radio and the record player to speakers in the crew's quarters and to the fantail area of the ship. A canvas awning had been rigged up over the entire fantail area, and this was a favorite hangout for those off-duty. Numerous records had been purchased while in Miami, but the favorite seems to have been "Tangerine," recorded with Helen O'Connell and Bob Eberly. It was played so often that I heard it even in my sleep. Easily we could have become known as the USS *Tangerine*.

To keep up our appearance, regular haircuts were a necessity. Barber shops were few and far between when small ships were involved. In Miami the ship acquired two sets of barbering equipment, which included hand clippers. Three crew members from small, midwestern rural towns had worked in barber shops cutting hair on Saturdays. They volunteered to keep the crew of the *SC-761* properly sheared. At regular intervals the officers and crew got a free, navy-style haircut while sitting on a crate or bucket under the awning on the fantail.

At mid-morning of 25 February, we crossed the equator. Members of a ship's company who have never crossed the equator are known as "Pollywogs." Those who have been across are called "Shellbacks." Ceremonies have always existed in the navy to initiate "Pollywogs" into the Ancient Order of the Deep. On the *SC-761* only Chester Stanley Choinski, GM2c, USN was a "Shellback." Thus, our ceremony was merely a formality. In jest, Choinski did have the yeoman type up charges he leveled against each member of ship's company. Don Terry, our yeoman, sent Margaret, his future bride, a copy of some of these fanciful charges and she has preserved some.

Among them were charges against the ship's cook, Al Sansfacon, and the mess attendant, J. P. Johnson, for not serving meals on time. Their punishment was to stand one watch as officer of the deck and assistant officer of the deck. T. J. Tarazska, EM1c, was charged with stealing and eating Feathers' food. His fine was to cook a steak for Feathers and feed it to the dog rather than eat it himself. J. A. Budzisz, SM2c, was charged with sending incorrect signals and belly-robbing the crew by eating too often. His punishment was to sit on the wherry and make certain no mermaid hitch-hiked a ride. Ensign Hannah was charged with wasting good food over the side whenever the sea got a little rough. He was required to stand his next watch with a long glass and side arms, wearing white gloves. Lieutenant Balcom was charged with keeping the ship at sea too long, which interfered with liberty for the crew. He had to see that all punishment meted out by Neptunus Rex at this ceremony was carried out properly. I was charged with poor navigation causing the SC-761 to miss an island destination by two moons, being only ninety-eight and seven-eighths degrees off course. I was to stand a lookout watch in shorts, with side arms and a long glass, while wearing a dress cap.

Each crew member was issued a card signed by Neptunus Rex, Ruler of the Raging Main, and by Davy Jones, His Majesty's scribe. Not only did the ceremony give a bit of levity to the daily routine we had been following, but also boosted the morale of the crew.

The only excitement was a possible submarine contact the late afternoon of 1 March. At 1750 the SC-760, with screening station on starboard bow of the convoy, signaled he had a good sound contact and was turning to a course of approximately fifty degrees true at flank speed. The entire convoy made an emergency turn of forty-five degrees to port and all hands went to general quarters. The escort commander detached two other subchasers, SCs-982 and 648 to assist. The SC-760 made two mousetrap attacks and one depth charge attack. While two of the mousetrap bombs exploded, no appreciable results came to surface. Apparently a school of large fish caused the ASW equipment to register the good sound contact mimicking that of a submarine. Nevertheless, the incident served to remind us that our convoy could well be enemy prey.

On Wednesday, 10 March, at 0855, land was sighted by the lookout. All hands came topside to witness the event. After twenty-one long days at sea, it was a welcome sight. By noontime we had a fine view of Bora Bora. ComSoPacFor ordered the Pecos to continue alone towards Noumea, since other escorts would meet it en route.

All remaining ships were to have a five-day break to recover

from the long journey in small ships. Therefore, the convoy began
to enter Teavanui Harbor at Bora Bora. This took some time as there
is only a narrow entrance through the coral reef which surrounds
the island. While the *SC-761* was lying to, awaiting its turn to enter,
several crew members asked the skipper to allow them to jump into
the beautiful, clear blue waters. Swimming call was granted after
Choinski was posted on the fantail with a rifle in case sharks appeared.
Several men jumped in and swam for a few minutes, climbing back
aboard when it came our turn to enter port. As we approached the
narrow passage through the coral reef, on the forecastle were posted
not only the special sea detail and a leadsman but also two "reef lookouts." Lying on their stomachs, their heads jutting over the side,
they looked down through the sparkling clear water. Wearing ear-
phones connected to the flying bridge, they were able to report on
the status of the coral reef. All ships cleared the harbor entrance
successfully.

Teavanui Harbor was created out of the bed of an extinct volcano. Eons ago one side of the volcano had fallen into the sea, providing an entrance for the ocean. Over time a coral reef had grown
up around the island, thus providing a well-protected harbor. It was
a magnificent sight as we entered the harbor, typical of what you
would expect of a South Sea island in a Hollywood movie. Lush tropical growth and large coconut trees abounded. There was no appearance of civilization other than a small naval outpost. At 1640 we
moored alongside the *SC-730*, which had anchored in fourteen fathoms of water. The *SC-641* was moored on the other side of the *SC-
730*. Thus, these three ships were nested together again.

At that time the navy had significantly reduced the number of
men stationed at Bora Bora. A commander was in charge. The men
stationed there were to assist small craft in refueling and obtaining
water at the one dock installed by the navy. I went ashore and met
the commander. Learning he suffered with a painful ulcer and was
unable to consume his beer ration, I made a trade with him. We still
had a half-dozen eggs left over from our trip, and he had not had any
for some time. Only dry rations were available at this small naval
outpost. He gave me three cases of beer for those old eggs. I notified
the ship, and the men came ashore in groups to enjoy a beer after
twenty-one days at sea.

The next day I took a working party of five ashore. We climbed
to the top rim of this old volcano covered with dense growth and
had a beautiful view of the entire area. Descending, we cut several
stalks of green bananas growing wild and carried them back to the

ship. We hung the stalks on the flying bridge to ripen in the sun. Those bananas were a welcome treat, the first fresh fruit we had available in weeks.

Margaret Terry has saved a note from Don Terry that contains a rough sketch of a previously unidentified island covered with palm trees. Don tells her the "island I sketch at dawn while on watch in the pilothouse belongs to Dorothy Lamour; that is, it fits in with her films in the sense of its beauty and splendor and its delightful climate." He could not have described it better, as Bora Bora at that time was unspoiled by civilization. Certainly no tourist had visited the island except, perhaps, by private yacht. A most refreshing five days were spent in this tropical paradise, which years later became the site for a Hollywood remake of the film classic, *Mutiny on the Bounty*.

Rejuvenated, we were ready to sail on to Noumea and join Admiral Halsey and the South Pacific Fleet.

CHAPTER 5

Bora Bora to Noumea

On 14 March Lieutenant McIlvaine called all commanding officers to a briefing conference ashore. At that meeting he detailed the procedure for continuing on to Noumea as per ComSoPac order 130230 of March 1943. He was to divide the remaining ships into four groups. Accordingly, he divided the LCIs into three groups, each to be escorted by three SCs. The remaining five YMSs, AT and YN along with two SCs comprised the fourth group. Each group was to sail at twelve-hour intervals beginning the next morning, with approximate twelve-hour stops in Pago Pago and Suva.

Promptly at 0800 on 15 March the first group, designated as Task Unit 36.4.1, got under way. The second group, designated as Task Unit 36.4.2, got under way at 2000. This group comprised five LCIs, the *SC-730*, the *SC-641*, and the *SC-761*. Our task unit commander was on board the *SC-730*.

Pago Pago is in the American Samoan Islands and has long been a naval base, where fuel, water, and some fresh supplies were readily available. It is only a relatively short trip of four days from Bora Bora. On 19 March at 0625 Tau Island was sighted, bearing 350 degrees true, distance about twelve miles. Just after lunch at 1330 we began to enter Pago Pago Harbor, allowing the LCIs to proceed first. Because each of the three SCs needed fuel and water, they tied up to the piers.

Having stayed only overnight, on 21 March at 1217 this group departed Pago Pago en route to Suva. After a slightly longer trip of almost five days, our task unit entered Suva Harbor in the Fiji Islands very early on the morning of 25 March. Fortunately, the SCs were able to anchor near King's Wharf close to the center of town. Suva was our first and only real liberty port since leaving Balboa

23

thirty-two days before. It was a very welcome spot for a crew confined so long to the 110 feet of the *SC-761*. Watch sections were revised and rotated so that three-fourths of the crew could be on liberty at any one time.

A very pleasant British town with shops, restaurants, and pubs made it a delightful spot for a short respite. British Cable & Wireless Company had an office on the main street, and I was able to send a cable notifying home that all was well. The cable did not indicate the place from which it was dispatched. There were very few military personnel then stationed at Fiji as most had moved out with the earlier Guadalcanal campaign.

Suva had all the comforts of British civilization including cricket and rugby fields, tennis courts, even a golf course. We did not have time to enjoy any of those amenities, but Jim Hannah and I scouted the area and discovered the stately Grand Pacific Hotel. A large white stone structure, it had a grand veranda forming a semicircle around the building. It was situated in the midst of beautiful gardens maintained with meticulous care.

As Jim and I climbed the few steps up to the veranda entrance we were greeted by a very pleasant, young native waiter. He was dressed in immaculate white clothes, but he was barefoot. Like most of the natives he disdained the wearing of shoes. Learning that the bar had scotch whiskey, Jim and I wasted no time ordering a drink. Sitting on the open veranda in these peaceful and beautiful surroundings, sipping our first drink since Balboa, made it difficult to imagine that the horrors of war in Guadalcanal were just over the horizon. It was our last truly civilized relaxation for months to come. Following a meal that was gourmet to us, we made our way back to the ship to tell Ronald Balcom what we had found in Suva. He promptly went ashore for a drink.

The next morning we took on fuel, water, and all types of fresh food, making preparations to get under way for Noumea, the territorial capitol of New Caledonia. The port director warned us about very strong currents that existed off the southeast tip of the island of New Caledonia. He told us several U.S. naval vessels had recently misjudged these currents and gone on the reef. Thus warned, our task unit stood out of the harbor, clearing its entrance buoy at 1430.

Three days later at 1325 on 29 March, we sighted New Caledonia, bearing five degrees true, distance about sixty-five miles. At 1625 we entered Bulari Pass to Noumea Harbor, and the *SC-730*, leading our column, took on the mandatory pilot. By 1930 we moored alongside the *SC-641* in Dumbean Bay. The *SC-730* was moored on the other side of the *SC-641*. Again these three ships were nested together.

Lieutenant Balcom decided to stay aboard, since he and Lieutenant McIlvaine of the *SC-730* and Lieutenant Taylor of the *SC-641* would have to report to Admiral Halsey's headquarters early the next morning. As a result, Jim Hannah and I were able to go ashore. Soon we learned that this was the opening night of the officers' club at Noumea, and we took it in along with fellow officers from the *SC-730* and *SC-641*. Glassware had not yet arrived, so old beer cans with the tops cut out served as glasses. Chit books had to be purchased from the mess treasurer since no cash was used for drinks or dinner. Opening night was a boisterous affair. With many ships from the fleet in port, the place was packed; the bar was jammed full of officers of all ranks.

The next morning the skippers of the three SCs went ashore and reported to Adm. Wm. F. Halsey and his chief of staff, Capt. Miles Browning. This was the headquarters for the Third Fleet, the South Pacific Force. These subchasers were to be parceled out among various bases. The *SC-730*, *SC-761*, *SC-641*, and *SC-982* were assigned to the Solomon Islands, becoming part of Task Force 31 then under the command of Rear Adm. R. K. Turner. Whether these four were picked for the Solomons because they had the most senior skippers or because Lieutenant McIlvaine had some choice and input due to his seniority is unknown. Two of these subchasers, the *SC-518* and *SC-760*, were sent to Espiritu Santo and would join us in Tulagi by midsummer. I have not been able to ascertain where the others were initially posted, but there was a rumor that one or two went to MacArthur in New Guinea.

Don Terry, our yeoman, also went ashore to the fleet post office. Inquiring about the *SC-761*, he was handed a sack of mail. Before departing Miami we each told friends, wives, and other relatives that we could be reached by addressing letters to us at the USS *SC-761* in care of the Fleet Post Office, San Francisco. When Don brought that mail back on board all faces lit up with big grins and joyful eyes. No better morale booster exists than a letter from back home. Ronald Balcom had letters from Merle Oberon and Gary Cooper. We learned that as a young man his employer, Atlas Corporation, had obtained control of RKO Pictures and had sent him to Hollywood for several months. Assisting in the reorganization of RKO, he met many movie stars. From then on, future mail calls included letters to him from various actors and actresses. If only the *SC-761* had been stationed in Long Beach, what an entree we would have had to glamorous Hollywood parties!

In the meantime we had ten days in Noumea for minor ship

maintenance so we were able to see something of the city. It was very French, since the island of New Caledonia was established as a French Penal Colony in the early 1860s. Now, in 1943, it had about thirty-thousand inhabitants, the greater portion of whom were of European descent. The larger native population lived in the countryside. Noumea was not as hospitable as Suva. I do not recall going to any shops, stores, or hotels although they were available. When ashore, we usually went to the officers' club, only occassionally walking around portions of the town.

Noumea was well known for its "Pink House." The French, seeing the great influx of American military personnel, almost entirely male in those days, had established a bordelo. Our marines from the 1st Division had popularized it both going to and returning from Guadalcanal in 1942. This large pink-colored house was situated on a hill just outside of the town, but it was clearly visible from town. Needless to say, it was quite popular. Not only was the fleet in and out of the harbor, but over 20,000 army troops were stationed outside of Noumea.

Joe Effinger and Jim Moore each recall its existence. Moore writes that he and three other men from the *SC-761* walked out to the "Pink House," but the "line was over a mile long, so we went to town and drank beer in a hotel bar." Joe Effinger, observing the "Pink House" from town, wrote that "it looked, for all the world, like an ant hill. All these little ants in dungarees lined up to go see the queen ant. One line going in, another coming out, with the Shore Patrol keeping order. The exit line had a mandatory stop at a PRO station maintained by navy hospital corpsmen." Rumor has it there was a shorter line for officers.

Some Frenchmen must have gotten very rich due to the popularity of this place. Other Frenchmen got rich selling beer and liquor to the fleet on liberty, as well as selling all manner of supplies to the military. In any event, Noumea supplied a last bit of liberty and relaxation before we entered the war zone.

CHAPTER 6

The Solomon Islands— Part I

On Friday afternoon 9 April Task Unit 32.6.2, consisting of *SC-730, SC-641, SC-761, SC-982,* and *LST 448,* hoisted anchor and was under way for Guadalcanal at 1530. After clearing the harbor, a northwesterly course was set so as to pass along the west coast of New Caledonia. Since we were escorting the LST our speed was set at only 9 knots. Again we were fortunate to have good weather and mild seas as we proceeded through an eastern portion of the Coral Sea.

Sailing through these beautiful waters, some feeling of apprehension mingled with our anticipation for we were not sure what to expect in the Solomons. We only knew what we had read about the bloody battles fought by the 1st Marine Division during most of the last half of 1942 whereby Guadalcanal was wrested from Japanese control.

Actually, the Guadalcanal campaign had been America's first strategic offensive. Although the Japanese had been turned back by the Battle of the Coral Sea, they did occupy Tulagi at that time. Realizing they needed an airfield, not merely the seaplane base at Tulagi, they began to construct one on Guadalcanal in June 1942. This would be a menace, and accordingly the 1st Marine Division made its first landing in early August. All of us had read of this while undergoing our training in the States. That original Japanese airstrip later became our famous Henderson Field.

We all knew we were proceeding to a very special area, one where Japan first had to give up and retreat from territory it had occupied. Guadalcanal had become a significant turning point in the South Pacific. We realized we would soon be participating in the elimination of Japanese from those areas of the Solomon Islands which they still controlled.

27

As we sailed to the west of the New Hebrides, skirted the eastern edge of the Solomon Sea, and passed around the southeastern edge of San Cristobal Island, our excellent weather continued. At dawn on 14 April we had our first glimpse of Guadalcanal in the distance. It had some very high mountain ridges and peaks and was covered with dense jungle. After navigating through Sealark Channel, we passed into Iron Bottom Sound. At 1300 our task unit anchored off of Lunga Point, opposite the Red Beach of 1st Marine fame. A couple of supply ships were unloading in the Lunga roadstead, being screened by two subchasers which had arrived with an earlier group in March. There was no port and no docks for Guadalcanal, so ships were off-loaded into LCTs and barges. Thus, supply ships and troop transports while anchored in open waters were sitting ducks for enemy submarines. We realized a portion of our duties would be the screening of supply ships and troop ships.

All commanding officers went ashore in an LCT and reported in to Admiral Turner and his staff for duty. Those headquarters were between Lunga Point and Koli Point, somewhat nearer Koli as I recall, and had the code name of Camp Crocodile. Commanding officers, sometimes with their executive officers, were to report here often in future months for orders and briefings regarding upcoming military engagements and plans. The *SC-730* and *SC-982* relieved the two subchasers then screening off Lunga Point, while the *SC-761* and *SC-641* were ordered to dock at Tulagi Harbor.

Tulagi is an excellent harbor on Florida Island, and only a short distance across Iron Bottom Sound from Guadalcanal. Entering through the submarine nets, the *SC-761* moored to a buoy in the harbor, and the *SC-641* tied up alongside. We had our first view of what was to be our home for some six months. The harbor is not large, but it is adequate to handle nine subchasers which were now to be stationed there. Already present, having arrived in March, were the *SC-504, SC-505, SC-521, SC-531,* and *SC-668.* Our four additions now made a squadron. Lieutenant McIlvaine, in the SC-730, senior in grade to all other skippers, became commander submarine chasers Solomons, duly relieving the prior senior officer in the *SC-505.*

On a peninsula on our port side as we entered the harbor there was a large dock known as Government Dock, built earlier by the British. That dock was near the base of a hill on which was situated Government House. Nearby the Seabees had constructed another supply dock known as Sturgis Dock. In the future we would tie up to those two docks to receive supplies. Tulagi had served as the seat of government for all of the Solomon Islands which had been a British Protectorate. But there had been no real town, only a tiny community prior to the war. Now it was strictly a U.S. Naval Base, with a base medical dispensary, supply facilities, a Seabee unit, and an outdoor movie screen.

Opposite and toward the rear of this harbor, on the main portion of Florida Island, was the PT Base where future President Jack Kennedy was then stationed. The Maltali River flowed into the rear of this harbor near the PT Base where the Seabees had built a large water dock. They had rigged up a water pipeline to this dock from the main springs that fed this river which arose in the nearby mountains. The USS *Niagara*, tender for the PT boats, stayed moored to part of this dock. In the future we made regular trips to this dock, either mooring to it or to the *Niagara*, to take on water. Water was so plentiful that we could wash the ship completely to eliminate all salt accumulations, as well as luxuriate ourselves with long showers. I don't believe any of us ever enjoyed a shower more than those long ones we had while the ship was tied up to the Tulagi water dock.

Florida Island had two other small harbors, Gavutu and Baranago, immediately southeast of Tulagi, but they were never used by the subchasers. Farther to the southeast, nearer to the eastern end of Florida Island, was Purvis Bay. It was a splendid anchorage, and big enough to hold cruisers and other large ships. In the spring of 1943 it was deserted, except when a subchaser that had a couple of days off duty would go there to relax. The crews could fish and swim. There was a small native-built dock that had large, overhanging coconut trees. Nearby was an abandoned native hut. No natives were on Florida Island since they had fled to San Cristobal and other islands when the Japanese first landed. The Americans had not allowed the natives to return since the war was in progress. That dock area became a favorite spot for our ship to moor, and the overhanging trees gave us protection by hiding us from the Japanese planes during the numerous and extensive air raids occurring from April through July.

Our primary function was escort duty and screening duty. The high command had made the decision to keep our destroyer forces away from the Guadalcanal area during daylight hours, with the exception of future invasions. Therefore, in the spring of 1943 the destroyers generally remained back at Espiritu Santo during daylight. At night the destroyers made trips up through New Georgia Sound, known as "The Slot," to engage enemy warships and interfere with enemy supply activities. Some fierce sea battles resulted from these activities; we heard of them through the grapevine. In that era, enemy aircraft did not have the sophisticated radar and detection equipment displayed by us in the recent Persian Gulf War, so darkness afforded destroyers significant protection. Since the slot was ringed by Japanese airstrips, daylight activities could be very precarious. The war diary of the *SC-730*, the log books of the *SC-641*, and the log books and war diary of the *SC-761* reflect thirty days of Japanese air raids on the Guadalcanal-Tulagi areas between 16 April and 27 July. On some of those days and nights there were two or three separate air raids. With destroyers at that time tending to stay away from this area during daylight hours, the smaller, and more expendable, subchasers took up the slack of screening for submarines.

The first assignment in this area for the *SC-761* involved screening ships unloading off Lunga Point and the Kukum Beach area. It was known as the Copper Patrol and was a twenty-four-hour operation since ships unloaded around the clock. Generally we spent three days on such a patrol, and upon relief the ship proceeded first to the Tulagi water dock and then to the fuel barge moored in the harbor. After obtaining fuel and water the ship retired to Purvis Bay for two days of relaxation. Tied up to that little native dock we had easy access to the shore. A photograph of the three officers was taken beside an abandoned native hut and is reproduced in this book.

There were no recreation facilities available. At times when we anchored or moored in Tulagi Harbor, the off-duty sections attended the movie run by the Seabees, or, if at the water dock, the movie which was shown at the PT Base. These movies were often abruptly halted when Condition Yellow was sounded to alert all hands of an incoming air raid. Men returned to the ship by the time Condition Red occurred, so that the ship could be at general quarters.

At this time, there were no athletic facilities, no beer hall, no officers' club at Tulagi or anywhere else on Florida Island. Our main recreation consisted of bull sessions on the fantail, reading books the ship had acquired in Miami, using the record player, and listening to Tokyo Rose on the radio. No American or British radio station could be picked up in the Solomons by our radio facilities. While we hee-hawed at the comments made by Rose, we enjoyed the American music she played. One day in the mail, our ship received two Coca-Cola game sets. The Coca-Cola Company sent special game sets to ships in the most forward areas. Each set contained a couple of decks of cards, a checkerboard with checkers and chessmen, a set of dominos, and a cribbage board. Those game sets were greatly appreciated and used often. As cards were blown overboard, dominos and checkers lost, we were soon down to the two sets of chessmen. The three officers and the quartermaster played chess and taught the others the game. Soon every man eagerly competed at chess, a game many of them might never have learned otherwise. The *SC-761* may have been one of the few ships in the navy in which all hands knew the game of chess and played it actively and avidly.

No gambling was tolerated on our subchaser, but there was an occasional poker game played by men on another ship and at the PT Base. The *SC-761* apparently had two pretty good poker players, as reflected by money orders contained in letters of Choinski GM2c and of Moore, now a coxswain, which officers noted during censor activities.

Our next duty was to lead and screen a convoy of LCTs from Guadalcanal to the Russell Islands. These small islands are located some thirty miles from Cape Esperance toward New Georgia and had been occupied by American forces since about February of 1943. A small airstrip was being constructed in preparation for the planned occupation of New Georgia. Furthermore, the Russells would be a staging area for any such invasion. Being in close proximity to Japanese airfields in the New Georgia area, major supply ships did not visit the Russell Islands. Usually all supplies were sent in the small LCTs, driven by a coxswain. The LCTs lacked any navigation equipment, having been designed to carry troops ashore from troop transports during an invasion. These LCTs would be loaded in the Lunga Point area during the early afternoon. Then around 1700 they shoved off from the shoreline. The duty subchaser would join them, taking the lead. Like ducklings, the LCTs, usually three to five in number, followed behind.

With a convoy speed of about 6 knots it took approximately two hours to reach the area between Cape Esperance and Savo Island. Once at that point of departure, we set a course of about 280 degrees true, as the Solomon Islands lie with an axis situated approximately northwest to southeast. It was then about seven more hours before we would reach the final destination in Renard Cove. It would be about 0200 before we could tie up to the small dock in Renard Cove so the LCTs could unload during the night. Once the LCTs discharged their cargo, we would start back to Guadalcanal with our brood about 0800, hoping no Japanese aircraft would appear during the daylight return trip. It would be around 1700 before we returned to Tulagi. Accordingly, each such trip involved at least twenty-four hours.

Outgoing trips began in the evenings so as to have the benefit of darkness. We quickly learned the LCTs had great difficulty following us after dark. As a result, we rigged a small red light astern, shielded in a tube pointed aft, so the lead LCT had a point of reference in the dark. Each LCT made a large wake visible to the next LCT immediately astern. Seeing such wake, one LCT could follow another and thus stay in column as long as the leading LCT was able to follow the *SC-761*. We had to be particularly careful to see that they properly entered Renard Sound and proceeded to Renard Cove without running aground.

Making these trips to the Russell Islands, screening the Lunga Point area in a Copper Patrol and the Koli Point area in a Champagne Patrol, responding to possible submarine sightings by our aircraft, and escorting an APC or LST to San Cristobal Island, to Ulawa Island, to Ugi Island and other such points in the Solomons constituted the major activities of this group of subchasers. Sometimes we had special screening duties encompassing areas around Savo Island. Here, as well as near Cape Esperance, our ASW equipment obtained good tests as we pinged off of the numerous hulks of American and Japanese warships which had been sunk in these waters in two ferocious naval battles in 1942. By virtue thereof the area between Guadalcanal and Florida Island acquired the name Iron Bottom Sound.

Our ships and the shore facilities in the Guadalcanal-Tulagi area were constantly harassed by Japanese air raids. Sometimes we were caught out in the middle of Iron Bottom Sound. Usually the few Japanese planes which got through our air cover sought to bomb and strafe the supply ships or facilities near Henderson Field or at Tulagi. However, on 16 June and again on 17 June, we experienced very heavy air raids. The air raid on 16 June was extensively reported three days later in the American press. J. Norman Lodge, a veteran Associated Press war correspondent, was an eyewitness to this attack. Apparently a large convoy of troopships unloading at Guadalcanal attracted the Japanese. Lodge in his AP dispatch reported:

> The Japanese tried one of the most crushing blows of the Pacific War today as 120 enemy planes of all types came over (Guadalcanal) .... After the smoke had cleared the Japanese had lost 45 Zeros and 32 dive bombers for six of our planes .... The enemy had left their bases under a screen of clouds they believed to extend as far southeast as Guadalcanal. However, when they arrived over Skylark Channel between Tulagi and Guadalcanal, clear skies greeted the sons of heaven and ack-ack from ships and shore batteries blasted the first wave of attackers into the ocean .... Our fighters came hurtling down from 20,000 feet, mixed like Donnybrook with the enemy and sent 32 Zeros into a fiery crash into the sea.

Throughout the United States the newspapers in bold headlines reported this military engagement in terms such as: "Great Air Battle Over Guadalcanal," "One Of Great Battles Of Pacific," or "U.S. Fliers Down 77 Jap Planes, All Time Record For Single Air Action."

On both the 16th and 17th, the *SC-761* and other subchasers were under way in the area between Tulagi and Guadalcanal. On the 16th no enemy planes came low enough to the *SC-761* to enable us to use our guns effectively. Fortunately, larger and more desirable targets were available to the Japanese, including troopships and an escort carrier. Nevertheless, the *SC-761* and the other subchasers were the object of attention by high-flying bombers. In each instance the *SC-761* had to make extremely quick zigzag maneuvers in open waters to avoid bombs dropped by Japanese planes. No subchaser was damaged, although bombs came very close to one or two of our sister ships. We were not strafed, but on the 17th one enemy plane came so low to us that J. P. Johnson, our mess attendant, stationed in a 20MM gun crew, recently told me that he still vividly recalls seeing the whites of the eyes of the pilot.

During that raid on the 17th our war diary reflects the expenditure of 139 rounds of 40MM and 420 rounds of 20MM with no known results. However, the war diary of the *SC-730* reflects that during the raid on the 17th the various subchasers hit two large, low-flying Japanese bombers with 20MM bursts, but neither plane crashed as a result. War correspondent J. Norman Lodge accounted for an LST as being the only significant casualty among the ships present.

Many times the *SC-761* was tied up to that small dock in Purvis Bay under cover of those overhanging coconut trees during the nighttime air raids. On those occasions we had a ringside seat and witnessed the ensuing antiaircraft fire, the tracers, and the searchlights on Guadalcanal used to repulse such raids. In a sense it was like a July 4th fireworks display. After having been a target during those two major daylight air raids, we enjoyed the luxury of being a hidden spectator.

During the midwatch on 19 June, while on screening patrol off Lunga Point, the *SC-761* struck a submerged object which damaged the underwater portion of its sonar gear. There was so much hidden debris floating underwater in the Iron Bottom Bay areas that the war diary of the *SC-730* reflects that it and the *SC-982* had subsequent similar occurrences. In fact the *SC-730* had a submerged log jammed in its starboard screw so badly that navy divers had to remove it, and the screw ultimately had to be replaced. It was the fate of the *SC-761* to have the first such experience. Since two other subchasers

were scheduled to go to Espiritu Santo for drydocking and maintenance, the commander of Task Force Thirty-one decided that the
SC-761 should proceed along with them. As result, our first foray
into the Solomon Islands ended with this brief sojourn to the New
Hebridies for repairs.

It would be a welcome respite.

CHAPTER 7

The Solomon Islands — Part II

Topping off our fuel and water tanks at Tulagi the afternoon of 20 June, the *SC-761* was ready to depart for Espiritu Santo for repairs. The next morning at 1125 we cast off our lines from the East Buoy in Tulagi Harbor, and proceeded to stand out of the harbor. Once clear of the submarine nets we fell into column formation behind the *SC-504* and *SC-668*. After an uneventful trip, the three subchasers arrived off Espiritu Santo shortly after dawn on Thursday, 24 June and entered Segound Channel. Entering the harbor at 0810 the *SC-761* was directed to go alongside the USS *Dixie*, a repair ship stationed at Espiritu Santo. Except for two short trips into the floating drydock, the USS *ARD 5*, the *SC-761* would remain alongside the *Dixie* for the sixteen days we were at Espiritu Santo. It was not easy to repair the sonar, but fortunately the *Dixie* had very skilled personnel with which to accomplish the task. Our crew assisted in every possible way. After a final trip to the *ARD 5*, everything was back in working order.

Espiritu Santo had much more to offer the crew than merely movies. There was an officers' club, a petty officers' club, and a general beer hall. In the evenings the off-duty sections frequented these facilities, as well as having a multitude of choices among showings of the latest movies. The officers' club claimed to have the longest bar in the navy. Good steaks, fresh vegetables, real eggs, and fresh milk were plentiful and a most welcome change from the dry rations which had been our general fare in the Solomons. Only occasionally in the Solomons were we able to requisition some fresh food from naval supply ships unloading in the Lunga roadsted. Even though our cook skillfully and imaginatively had made various dishes out of Spam, they still tasted like Spam. Furthermore, powdered eggs and dehydrated potatoes had been merely tolerated at best. So the fresh meat and real eggs available at Espiritu Santo were a luxury we savored those sixteen days. Even milkshakes and ice cream were eagerly devoured. Things we had taken for granted in the States were now fully and truly appreciated. At Espiritu Santo we lost two very capable petty officers. The *Dixie* personnel who worked with T. J. Tarazska EM1c and P. B. Pullen RM2c, decided the *Dixie* could better use their skills. From the receiving station we now received James F. McKnight EM3c, who turned out to be a fine addition to the crew. This began a trend of transfers over the ensuing eighteen months as personnel were promoted.

On 1 May, after departing Balboa, Ronald Balcom was promoted to lieutenant. Among the crew, Burrell became QM1c, Budzisz SM1c, Grimm S1c, Groeschel S1c, Grove MoMM1c, Hightower SoM2c, Johnson MAtt 1c, McMullen M0MM2c, Moore S1c, Pullen RM2c, Sansfacon SC1c, Singer MoMM1c, Terry Y1c, Wootten SoM2c, and Vandergriff F1c. All were very capable personnel, well equipped for their rates. In fact the *SC-761* was most fortunate in the quality of personnel it received from time to time. Unfortunately we did not receive a replacement for Pullen until after we returned to Guadalcanal, where Leon Netka RM2c, another excellent addition to ship's company, came aboard as a transfer from the naval radio facilities in the Russell Islands.

With all repairs and maintenance completed, after swinging ship and running the degaussing range, the *SC-761* began its solo trip back to Tulagi in the early afternoon of Sunday, 11 July. Two mornings later we overtook the *LST 460* and four YPs en route to Guadalcanal via Ugi Island. The LST (SOPA) requested that we screen her and the YPs to Ugi Island some forty miles distant where they were taking some supplies to the seaplane base at Selwyn Bay.

Shortly thereafter, we came upon a crashed navy seaplane, a portion of which was floating above water. We noted that the wrecked plane had two depth charges attached to its wings. The LST knew this, as well as the fact that those two depth charges had live settings and had been directed to destroy the plane. We were now ordered to accomplish that destruction using one of our depth charges, set on fifty feet. It was fired from our starboard K-Gun, scoring a direct hit. Our exploding depth charge caused the wreckage to sink, and the two live depth charges then exploded simultaneously. The column of water blown up into the air by the three depth charges reminded me of the geysers at Yellowstone National Park.

We arrived at Selwyn Bay, Ugi Island, about 1530 on 13 July where we remained until almost midnight of the next day when the convoy was finally unloaded. During the interim we had time to go ashore. Feathers, our mascot, went along with some of us. The dog had not been able to leave the ship at Espiritu Santo, so he now enjoyed a jaunt on dry land. A photograph of the native chief at Ugi, his relatives and retinue, along with two junior officers from the LST is among the pictures in this book.

Departing at 2325 on 14 July, we escorted the LST and the four YPs to Guadalcanal. Shortly after noontime of the 15th, we arrived at Koli Point, Guadalcanal, left our convoy and crossed over to Tulagi. Mooring to the East Buoy in the harbor, we were back home.

Visiting with fellow officers from the subchasers which had remained in the Solomons, we heard details of the New Georgia invasion. That invasion began the evening of 21 June, the same day we had departed for Espiritu Santo, and continued until 5 July. We also learned of two fierce naval battles: (1) Kula Gulf, 8 July, when the USS *Helena* was sunk, and (2) Kolombangara, which encompassed two days, 12–13 July. With the invasion of New Georgia, Purvis Bay was no longer deserted. A few major elements of the fleet now used it as their base of operations.

Soon the subchasers would share Tulagi Harbor with two submarines. This area as well as the type of ships using it had begun to change. At this time we did not realize that following the upcoming invasion of Vella LaVella and the subsequent preparations for the invasion of Bougainville, the types and quantities of ships using Purvis Bay would change even more. In fact, by mid-September Purvis Bay became so crowded that a harbor master was necessary. After our return from Espiritu Santo, subchasers at Guadalcanal-Tulagi were no longer alone during daylight hours.

Our return on 15 July coincided with Rear Adm. T. S. Wilkinson relieving Rear Adm. R. K. Turner as commander of Task Force Thirty-one and the Third Amphibious Force. Accordingly, the next afternoon when the *SC-761* took up screening position at Lunga Point for a Copper Patrol, Lieutenant Balcom briefly went ashore and made a courtesy call on Admiral Wilkinson. Through members of his staff we learned that Admiral Wilkinson had been an early advocate of the concept of leapfrogging around enemy positions. Apparently, action by Allied forces in the Solomons would now accelerate following the recent New Georgia invasion.

No sooner had the *SC-761* obtained fuel and water at Tulagi after completing Lunga patrol than it was ordered to investigate an underwater contact between Cape Esperance and Savo Island. The *SC-641* and *SC-531* joined in this search. For a day and a half these three subchasers conducted a systematic search covering an area thirty miles by twenty miles from Savo Island to the Russell Islands. All results were negative, so we were ordered back to Lunga Point for another Copper Patrol.

Completing this screening, on 24 July the commanding officer was directed to report to Admiral Wilkinson for special orders. After going ashore at Koli Point at noon, he was in conference at Camp Crocodile for nearly three hours. Accompanying him when he returned aboard were Commander Tyree and Captain Burke who had been at the briefing. Burke later became known as "31-knot Burke" and was ultimately promoted to vice-admiral. We took them to Tulagi, where their ships were docked. Only the skipper knew what was involved, but the rest of us realized something was at hand. Topping off with fuel and water, we then moored to the East Buoy. Our skipper told us to be ready to get under way the next morning.

Promptly at 1100 on Sunday, 25 July, we cast off from the buoy, stood out of the harbor, and proceeded alone toward the Russell Islands. Lieutenant Balcom now advised us that the *SC-761* had been selected by Admiral Wilkinson as the subchaser to carry out a highly secret mission. We would rendezvous after midnight with the USS *Guardfish* to bring back the first group of coastwatchers from Bougainville. We were to expect about fifteen passengers which the *Guardfish* would transfer to us on the high seas. This rendezvous was to occur at a location five miles south of Point Pleasant, Rendova Island.

Early Monday, 26 July, at 0355 we had a radar contact with the *Guardfish* as it surfaced on schedule seven miles away. Due to the rolling sea, we each moved to the lee side of Rendova. Coming alongside the *Guardfish* we commenced the transfer of passengers at 0510. This consumed thirty minutes, as fifty-nine persons, rather than fifteen, many of whom were Chinese, came aboard! Comdr. Norvell G. Ward (later promoted to rear admiral), who had just taken command of the *Guardfish* about ten days earlier, told us most of them had helped our coastwatchers avoid the Japanese. He did not want to abandon them to the enemy. Therefore, he continued sending his rubber raft back to the Bougainville coastline until all fifty-nine were aboard the *SC-761*.

Recently contacting Admiral Ward about the unusual number of passengers involved in that exchange, he has written: "I was surprised, yet I wasn't surprised. I thought I was going to have about 25 passengers, coastwatchers and native scouts who were being hunted by the Japs. But as they approached the beach, they collected other natives like a dog collects fleas. My not being surprised was because it was a repeat story of the *Gato* pick-up in Teop (earlier) in March while I was its executive officer."

With fifty-nine new passengers, both the *Guardfish* and the *SC-761* were overloaded. Passengers were all over the deck. Lt. Comdr. John R. Keenan of the Royal Australian Navy was in charge of them. Of the passengers, his coastwatchers consisted of about twenty men of the Australian/New Zealand armed forces, several local natives, and two or three Fijians. These native scouts were recruited by the Australian forces to assist the coastwatchers in their struggle to avoid the Japanese and survive in the jungles.

It was at 0540 when we bid adieu to the *Guardfish* and began our trip back to Guadalcanal. All of the passengers were hungry and tired, but cheerful. I asked Frenchie, our cook, what we might feed those fifty-nine guests. He replied, "Now we can get rid of all of that canned salmon." He was referring to the fact that we were always required to take salmon each time we drew dry stores from any naval supply facility. The crew detested it so we had salmon stored everywhere, even in some bilges. With so many passengers the cook needed help; Mr. Keenan got several Chinese to assist. Neither Frenchie nor the Chinese understood each other's language, but hand signals worked. We served several cases of canned salmon and lots of rice. When it was all over, the Chinese meticulously cleaned the galley, as well as all plates and utensils. They even cleaned the aft crew's quarters where they had eaten. Oh, how our cook wished he could keep two or three as extra hands!

Mr. Keenan took great delight in consuming a pot of hot tea, while relaying some of his experiences. In the jungle of Bougainville they were constantly on the move as Japanese would home in on his radio broadcasts. As he and his forces moved through the jungle with their native troops, he had run across Chinese who had been storekeepers on Bougainville and who had fled to the jungles when the Japanese first invaded. They had been most helpful in evading the enemy search groups, so he wanted to save them by bringing them back with him. Commander Ward of the *Guardfish* had the same compassion.

After the Australian/New Zealand coastwatchers had showered, shaved and eaten, they gathered on the forecastle for a photograph taken from our flying bridge. My research uncovered that photograph now reproduced herein. It was after sunset when we arrived back at

Lunga Point and moored to a recently installed buoy. Comdr. Price
Jones of the Royal Australian Navy came aboard and took charge of
transferring our passengers ashore. We remained moored at Lunga
overnight as our skipper was to report in to operations at Admiral
Wilkinson's headquarters the next morning. Again, he received secret
orders.

After going to Tulagi for water and fuel on the 28th, once more
we were under way on 29 July for another special mission. Lieutenant Balcom told us we would have a similar rendezvous at the same
location with the *Guardfish*. Promptly at 0345 we established radar
contact with the *Guardfish* as it surfaced, proceeded to the lee of
Rendova Island, and accomplished the transfer of passengers. This
time there were only twenty-two persons. Again, we disposed of
more canned salmon and rice. Returning our passengers to Lunga
Point, we moored there overnight.

The next morning the *SC-761* was under way for Koli Point as
our skipper again was to report to operations. On this occasion he
was personally commended by Admiral Wilkinson for accomplishing
these special missions. At the same time, by blinker, the ship received the following message from Admiral Wilkinson:

> 301218 Gr 17 BT Both were seaman-like jobs performed by a smart
> ship X Well done to all hands X Wilkinson X.

Each man on the ship felt very proud to have been a part of
these two missions and that they were serving on the USS *SC-761*,
selected by the admiral to accomplish same. The *Cotlant Newsletter*
of 18 September 1943 had an article regarding two SCs and two PCs
which had received special recognition in the Atlantic and the Pacific. The lead story stated: "The USS *SC-761* which has been operating in the Southwest Pacific, recently was assigned two special missions under the command of Adm. T. S. Wilkinson. Upon the completion of these missions the following message from Admiral Wilkinson
was received by the ship, commanded by Lt. Ronald B. Balcom,
USNR." Then the newsletter article quoted the above message ver-
batim.

We made one more such special mission on 28 August with the
USS *Greenling*. The submarine had injected and removed a military
scouting party from the Treasury Islands located about forty miles
southwest of Bougainville. Such operation concluded the removal of
the coastwatchers from Bougainville and the scouting party from
Treasury Island prior to invasion. The story concerning these
coastwatchers and their significant contributions to the Allied cause

is detailed in a very interesting book, *Lonely Vigil: Coastwatchers of the Solomons,* by Walter Lord (Viking Press, 1977). However, it fails to identify the subchaser involved. Heretofore, only a detailed research of official navy records in the National Archives and at the Naval Historical Center at the Washington Navy Yard would have revealed such subchaser was our own proud USS *SC-761.* Why we were selected is not known. Other subchasers could have accomplished the same missions. We felt most honored that Admiral Wilkinson had chosen us from the fleet of subchasers then under his command in the Solomons.

Other types of operations now awaited us.

CHAPTER 8

The Solomon Islands — Part III

During the month of August the tempo of military activity increased significantly in our area. We now began operating with one or more destroyers to resupply our troops at New Georgia and its ajoining island of Rendova. Rendova lies immediately southwest of New Georgia, separated by the narrow Blanche Channel. Our troops had landed on Rendova on 30 June, following the initial landings on New Georgia a few days earlier. Usually LSTs were used to carry supplies and any relief troops. On 4 August the *SC-761* and the *DD 407* convoyed two loaded LSTs from Kukum Beach near Lunga Point to Rendova Harbor in Blanche Channel. We all departed Kukum shortly after noon, traveling at the slow LST speed of 9 knots. By the time we passed the area of the Russell Islands, it was dusk. Therefore, most of the trip was made under the cover of darkness, and we arrived at Rendova Harbor just before sunrise. Once the LSTs were safely beached the destroyer retired from the area and the *SC-761* made antisubmarine sweeps of Blanche Channel. We had to be extremely alert for enemy aircraft as well as submarines.

It was about 1800 before the LSTs were ready to return to Guadalcanal. By that time the destroyer returned and our convoy departed near dusk. This gave our convoy the benefits of night while traveling within and near much of the New Georgia-Rendova area. Our group arrived back at Kukum Beach about midafternoon. The entire operation involved some forty-eight hours over portions of three days. A similar convoy trip was made on 10–11 August, but this time we were accompanied by the DD 406 instead of the DD 407.

No sooner had we retired at 1840 to our favorite mooring buoy in Tulagi Harbor, when we again received special orders. This time the *SC-761* and its sister ship from Ipswich, the *SC-760*, were to be part of the screen for the initial invasion of Vella LaVella. Again, Admiral Wilkinson chose us, and, as it turned out, this seems to have been the first time a subchaser was used in this type of mission. At midnight we were under way for Koli Point for our detailed assignments under the operations order. Receiving them, we proceeded to the Kukum Beach area of Guadalcanal, where we were joined by the *SC-760*, then commanded by Lt. (jg) G. P. Poor. After sunset the evening of the 12th, the two subchasers departed Kukum, escorting the *LST 395* to Renard Cove in the Russell Islands. There it could take on some special equipment and personnel. Shortly after dawn on 13 August, our convoy entered Renard Sound. Once the *LST 395* moored to the dock in Renard Cove, we tied up alongside, while the *SC-760* anchored nearby in the Sound.

While we were in the Koli Point-Kukum Beach area on the 12th, we observed the task force being assembled for the pending invasion. The *SC-641*, one of the subchasers which had been with us since Miami, was part of the screen for those ships engaged in the loading and unloading of men and materiel. Warner Keeley, Jr., of Pebble Beach, California, then a lieutenant, junior grade, was the executive officer of that subchaser at that time. He has furnished me with an extensive tape recording regarding the sinking of the *John Penn*, a troopship, on 13 August. He was on watch on the flying bridge of the *SC-641* when he observed some of our planes, with their lights on, returning to Guadalcanal from an air raid on Japanese bases. The planes were emitting proper identification signals with their IFF equipment. Suddenly, a nearby screening destroyer opened fire with its antiaircraft battery, and Warner, in amazement, exclaimed to his fellow crewmen, "My God, that destroyer is trying to shoot down our own planes."

But such was not the case. The destroyer had excellent radar and identification equipment, and was able to ascertain that a group of Japanese planes were following directly behind our returning planes. Our pilots had not realized they were being followed, but the destroyer was able to tell something was wrong and began firing at these other planes. Our aircraft flew on past Henderson Field and then everyone opened fire. At least one of the Japanese aircraft was a torpedo plane, and Warner witnessed it launch a torpedo towards the *SC-641*. Quickly maneuving the *SC-641*, he saw the torpedo pass directly by the fantail, missing the ship by inches. The torpedo then struck the *John Penn*, a violent explosion ensued, and the *John Penn* sank, losing much of its crew.

Warner had seen the troops on *John Penn* unload earlier, as those men were to be embarked on other landing craft for the invasion. Thus, the loss of life was limited to only members of the crew. For days thereafter, bodies of sailors would float to the surface of the waters at the Lunga roadstead, and the screening subchasers would notify authorities ashore. In turn, an LCT would be dispatched to pick up the body or bodies. Don Terry, the yeoman on the *SC-761*, tells me he still has an occasional dream about the ghastly sight of those floating, bloated bodies off Guadalcanal.

Being in the Russell Islands, the *SC-761* missed that action the night of 13 August. However, our war diary reflects we had a Condition Red at 0205 on 14 August and manned our general quarters stations for a short time. Apparently, some of those enemy planes flew near the Russell Islands while returning to their home bases.

Spending approximately twenty-four hours at Renard Cove, the *SC-761* and the *SC-760* departed with the loaded LST at 0800 on 14 August. At 1015 we rendezvoused at designated Point Baker with two destroyers, USS *Conway* and USS *Eaton*, and *LST 354* and *LST 399*. Our part of the invasion group consisted of the two destroyers and these two subchasers as the screen, and those three LSTs as the transport group. The LSTs were in column formation with the *Conway* on the port bow, the *Eaton* on starboard bow, the *SC-761* on starboard quarter and the *SC-760* on the port quarter of the convoy.

Admiral Wilkinson had organized three landing groups, each with screening ships. The main group contained the *Dent, Kilty, McKean, Stringham, Talbot, Ward,* and *Waters* as troop transports. Its screen comprised the destroyers *Chevalier, Cony, Nicholas, O'Bannon, Pringle,* and *Taylor.* Being the fastest ships, this group departed last from Guadalcanal. The second group had twelve LCIs, loaded with troops, together with the destroyers *Philip, Renshaw, Saufley,* and *Waller* for a screen. This group was faster than our LSTs, so it departed Guadalcanal after our group but prior to the main group.

After clearing the Savo Island-Cape Esperance area, these first two groups sailed out into the eastern edges of the Solomon Sea passing west of the Russell Islands. They caught up with the slower group two hours or so prior to reaching the approaches to Vella LaVella. Following the invasion route, all groups in the landing order specified departed the Solomon Sea and proceeded north with Ganongga Island to port, Gizo Island to starboard. In proper landing sequence they passed through Gizzo Strait into the Vella Gulf, their final destination being Barakoma Beach, on the southeastern side of Vella LaVella. The groups were scheduled to arrive at the Barakoma Beach area one group immediately after the other. The landings were made in three relatively quick stages by the first group, second group, and third group in that order.

When our group was about about thirty miles from Gizo Strait at 0305 the first two groups, one only a very short distance behind the other, began to overtake us to seaward on our port side. In the darkness, to our crew standing by their general quarters stations with helmets affixed and wearing life jackets, it looked like a mighty armada. Because the *SC-761* had not seen or been involved with anything like this operation, our blood tinged with excitement. We knew Admiral Wilkinson was embarked in the *Cony,* but his flag was not visible in the darkness. The main group began landing men on Barakoma Beach as dawn broke. Next came the second group with the LCIs moving in as close as possible to the beach, enabling troops to wade ashore. Then followed our slower group with the LSTs, which were able to beach themselves and unload equipment of all types for combat troops.

Pursuant to the operations order the two subchasers were directed to make an antisubmarine screen in Gizo Strait to protect the flank of the landing forces. The *SC-761* was directed to patrol the northwest end of Gizo Strait, nearer Barakoma Beach; the *SC-760* patrolled the southeast end, towards Rendova. While conducting this screening operation, the first wave of Japanese planes attacked the landing forces and the ships. Our war diary reflects the first attack was made by dive bombers at 0758. Although the screening ships put up much antiaircraft fire, no results were recorded in our war diary. In addition, the *Conway* and the *Eaton* laid down smoke screens as part of the defense. Because there were numerous larger and more desirable targets, only two planes made a run on the *SC-761.* As we wildly zigzagged in Gizo Strait, firing our 40MM gun, two small bombs landed about fifty yards on our starboard beam, and a cluster of small bombs landed about 100 to 200 yards on the starboard bow. We did not notice any damage to these two planes from our gun, and the *SC-761* experienced no damage. The log for the *SC-760* reflects that it had a brief encounter with one enemy plane which flew some 5,000 feet overhead. The subchaser expended seventeen rounds of 40MM ammunition with no known results. The *SC-760* likewise suffered no damage. Some LCIs and perhaps one LST were bombed and strafed, but our war diary does not reflect the actual extent of injury.

At 0940 elements of the first and second transport groups along with their screens cleared by us as they passed through Gizo Strait, returning to Guadalcanal. Soon thereafter our two destroyers began their return trip. Apparently, the LSTs would unload all day, and the two subchasers were directed to proceed independently to Rendova Harbor. Arriving there we met the *SCs 733* and *505*, the *LST 472* and a seagoing tug. The *SC-733* and *SC-505* had escorted some LSTs to the Blanche Channel area the prior day and night and thus happened to be in the nearby area.

In any event, the *SC-761* along with three other subchasers proceeded to escort the *LST 472* and the tug back toward Guadalcanal, departing Rendova Harbor at 1933. This afforded us the cover of darkness for most of the trip. Shortly after dawn on 16 August the tug left this convoy and sailed into Renard Sound at the Russell Islands. According to orders, at noon our subchaser and the *SC-505* broke off from the convoy at Point Able and proceeded into Tulagi Harbor, while the *SC-760* and *SC-733* continued to escort the *LST 472* to the Kokum Beach area of Guadalcanal.

It had been an extremely busy and exciting week for us on the *SC-761*. We were proud to have been a part of this invasion; as far as we understood, this was the first time subchasers were employed in this manner in the Pacific. Eventually, through SCTC, some of us learned that subchasers thereafter were used extensively in the invasions involving The Marshalls, Eniwetok, Guam, Saipan, and Iwo Jima. But the *SC-761* and our sister ship, the *SC-760*, seem to have been the first, at least in the Pacific.

Entering Tulagi Harbor, our adrenaline was still flowing, and we were still a little hyper when we tied up to our favorite dock, the East Buoy. We welcomed the fact that we would have time to clean up the ship as well as ourselves. The invasion landings were successful — a good beachhead had been established. But we realized that soon it would be our turn to escort LSTs to Vella LaVella or Rendova for resupply purposes and to bring back wounded. In the meantime other subchasers would do this for a few days while we took it easy and relaxed a bit.

On 11 August the USS *Argonne*, a tender and repair ship, had arrived at Purvis Bay, and other major elements of the fleet followed likewise after the invasions of New Georgia and Vella LaVella. It was very helpful to have the *Argonne* so handy, since we often had trouble with our radar. The *SC-761* was authorized to have an ABK identification system; therefore, on 20 August we went alongside the *Argonne* and obtained such an installation. This work was completed late on 21 August, and we were once again ready for duty.

In short order the *SC-761* joined the USS *Waters* and USS *Stringham* to convoy one LST and three LCIs to Rendova Harbor, followed by that last special previously mentioned operation with the USS *Greenling* on 28–29 August. This military scouting party from the Treasury Islands included twelve officers, eight enlisted, and four natives and enabled us to dispose of the final case of canned salmon we had on board.

On 30 August we transferred C. A. Gardiner, RdM2c, back to the States to enter the V-12 program. Lieutenant Balcom had recommended Gardiner for this officer candidate program. Later, in January we would transfer G. E. Wootten, SoM2c, for the same program by virtue of a recommendation that I subsequently made when I became commanding officer. Therefore, two men from the crew of the *SC-761* were accepted into this program.

Much of September and the early part of October were spent with escort duty taking convoys of LSTs and LCIs to Rendova Harbor and to Vella LaVella. Usually we had one or two destroyer types with us, from among the *Talbot, Crosby, Hovey, Dent, Foote,* and others. These ships and other members of the fleet were now using Purvis Bay as an anchorage. Even Admiral Merrill's cruisers put in appearances. Tulagi was now also a submarine base, with the *Guardfish, Gato,* and *Greenling* operating therefrom.

One of our new duties was to escort an arriving submarine from an area between the Russell Islands and Savo Island into Tulagi. Before dawn a sumarine would surface at a designated spot; we would pick it up on our radar screen and rendezvous with it. This escort was necessary, otherwise our own planes would have attacked any surfaced submarine in these areas. As a result we became well acquainted with the officers and men of the *Guardfish* and the *Gato* in particular.

Previously discussed air raids still continued, but now mainly in the most forward areas. They were almost nonexistent in the Guadalcanal-Tulagi area. Air raids were a real hazard while at Rendova or Vella LaVella. The *SC-761* was fortunate to escape injuries or damage as it was seldom an object of attack. We never filed any action reports; most subchasers did not realize such reports were required. Generally only war diary entries were made. However, the *SC-505* did file a lengthly action report concerning the attack upon it off Barakoma Beach at Vella LaVella the morning of 21 August. Along with two destroyers, the *SC-505* had convoyed some LSTs to Barakoma in resupply operations for our troops on Vella LaVella. As we found customary, especially at Barakoma, once the LSTs were beached the destroyers hightailed it out of the area, with a lonely subchaser left during the day to screen for submarines.

While researching at the Naval Historical Center in the Washington Navy Yard, I read the action report of the *SC-505* concerning this attack. It stated that the subchasers were "expendable!" Such action report and its endorsements are included in the appendix. The Third Endorsement by Admiral Wilkinson explains this policy. The report of the raid on the *SC-505* by six of the thirty-five enemy planes is a clear statement of the type of hazards encountered by subchasers in the Solomons. Whenever the SC-761 was involved, fewer enemy planes got through our air cover, and those few generally attacked the LSTs and supply facilities ashore. As I said before, on the *SC-761* we were most fortunate indeed.

While in Tulagi on Sunday afternoon, 19 September, our commanding officer and executive officer were directed by Admiral Wilkinson's staff to come to Camp Crocodile for a special conference. Commander Ward of the *Guardfish* and Commander Foley of the *Gato* had received similar instructions. As we were all in Tulagi Harbor, the *SC-761* gave these two submarine skippers a lift to Guadalcanal. Arriving at 1320 off Koli Point, Commander Ward, Commander Foley, Lieutenant Balcom, and I went ashore for our respective conferences at the operations center. These conferences concerned the projected invasion of Bougainville. The instructions for Commander Ward and Commander Foley were extremely important. Admiral Ward, formerly Commander Ward, has written to me regarding his conferences, stating:

> Your story of 19 and 20 September events enables me to recover information I could not remember. I knew *Guardfish* was in Tulagi then, and that I had gone over to Guadalcanal ... to receive a briefing from the Marines about my mission in the vacinity of Empress Augusta Bay. Bob Foley was being briefed on a similar one for the East Coast of Bougainville. We were back over the next day for more detailed briefings with the reconnaisance teams we were to insert and extract ... Meanwhile *Guardfish* was cleaning its Torpedo Rooms by off-loading torpedoes and hauling equipment to receive the Marines' gear. I departed Tulagi, inserted my team near Cape Torokina, and extracted them ten days later for return to Tulagi. Then we departed on patrol. Approximately a month later I returned to Tulagi, picked up the same team and inserted them at Cape Torokina three days prior to the Amphib landing.

These two submarines and the specially trained marine teams they "inserted," "extracted" and "inserted" again played a significant part in the invasion of Bougainville. Unfortunately, the *SC-761* was not able to take part in that invasion, but the *SC-641* and others which had been with us in Tulagi did so. In fact Warner Keeley, Jr., who had been promoted to lieutenant, had become the commanding officer of the *SC-641*, and his ship took an active part in screening the flank of the landing areas at Empress Augusta Bay two days after the initial landings. A photograph taken of Lieutenant Keeley with a group of natives on San Cristobal Island appears with the other photographs in this book.

It was on that afternoon of 19 September, while the above four officers were in these conferences, that the *SC-761* was involved in an unusual and dramatic rescue mission. Ensign Hannah was left in charge of the ship. At 1510 one of our large bombers was observed skimming across the water and suddenly crashing about three miles off Koli Point. The *SC-761* was the only ship in the immediate area. Ensign Hannah radioed for medical assistance and rescue equipment, and at flank speed raced to the site of the crashed plane. The crew of the plane was floating in the water. The men of the *SC-761* fished these survivors from the water and laid them on the deck. Soon a destroyer, the *DD 383*, answering the radio request of Hannah, sped into the area. Mr. Hannah signaled: "Do you have a doctor aboard?" Receiving an affirmative reply, he then signaled: "I am coming alongside, critically need doctor and corpsmen." And without hesitation, or even explicit permission, he went alongside.

Dr. Kabeisern and his corpsmen clambered aboard the *SC-761* with oxygen tanks and other equipment and began tending to the wounded. The doctor declared one man dead, who was stretched out on the deck amidships, his head split open and his brains oozing onto the deck. Only one man seemed to be uninjured, he would not lie down. In the chart room he gave the quartermaster the names of all the men and their duty station, and this data was entered in the rough log. The plane had returned from a raid on Japanese facilities at Rabaul where it had been heavily damaged. It almost, but not quite, made it back to Henderson Field. Boats soon came out from shore; one took the dead airman, another took the living survivors. We later heard that the one man who displayed no injuries, and who would not heed the doctor's warning to lie down, keeled over dead as he walked ashore. Perhaps it was from fright, we shall never know. In the midst of all this, Lieutenant Balcom and I, accompanied by the two submarine skippers, returned aboard from the conferences at Camp Crocodile, and the *SC-761* returned to Tulagi.

Once Lieutenant Balcom was apprised of what had occurred, he recorded a commendation to Ens. James B. Hannah for "his excellent handling of the ship, direct communications, and speed with which he procured doctors and ambulance service ashore." Inserted in their service records were special commendations to *Choinski*, Chester Stanley, GM1c, and *Grimm*, Randall Stevens, GM3c, "for their expertness in rendering first aid."

After another convoy run to Munda with the USS *Foote (DD 511)* on 21–23 September, we again returned to Tulagi. Then on 28 September, Ens. Joseph F. Effinger USNR, reported on board for duty as the new third officer. Likewise, orders were received whereby Lt. R. B. Balcom USNR was to be relieved of command by me, and Ens. James B. Hannah USNR was appointed executive officer of the USS *SC-761*. This was pursuant to ComSoPac file P16-4/00/(06), Serial 9952p, and by ComSoPac file P16-4/00/(06), Serial 9958p, each dated 17 September 1943. The necessary files having been checked, the proper papers for change of command having been executed, the crew was called to quarters on the quarterdeck. Lieutenant Balcom read his orders, and in turn I read mine. Thereupon, saluting Lieutenant Balcom, I said, "I relieve you sir, and hereby assume command of the *SC-761*."

At twenty-two years of age, younger than most of my crew, I assumed responsibility for those men and that ship — not stateside, but at Tulagi! In wartime one shoulders serious responsibilty very early in life. In order to appear older, I had even grown a moustache, and retained it until I returned to the States. I was indeed proud to assume command of this ship and its fine complement of personnel.

Early the next morning we were under way for Lunga Point. Once there, a motor launch came alongside and took Lieutenant Balcom ashore for further transfer back to the States and advanced training at SCTC in Miami. He had his sea chest shipped to Gary Cooper in Hollywood since he expected to spend his thirty days' leave with his friends in the film capital. The ship then proceeded to Koli Point, where I went ashore and paid my respects to Admiral Wilkinson. That formality accomplished, the *SC-761* returned to Tulagi and moored to its favorite buoy. Now another chapter in the saga of the *SC-761* would begin.

For the next three weeks our routine remained the same. Convoy trips to New Georgia, Rendova, and Vella LaVella constituted our main activities. On the final trip to Barakoma Beach, Vella LaVella, one of the unloading LSTs was badly bombed. A tug attempted to take the LST in tow but it was so badly damaged that once in deep water it began to sink almost instantly. We watched the drama as the crewmen on the tug feverishly worked to cut the towing cable with an acetylene torch so that the tug would not be pulled under. Fortunately, they acted just in time. Seconds made a lot of difference.

The occupation of New Georgia and Vella LaVella had made it impossible for the Japanese to continue supplying any of its remaining troops in the New Georgia area. The efforts to remove their troops from Kolombangara prompted the Battle of the Vella Gulf. This was a destroyer battle and occurred over the nights of 6 and 7 October. In spite of heavy injuries inflicted on the Japanese forces, our *Chevalier* was sunk, and the *Selfridge* and the *O'Bannon* were so damaged they would have to return to the States. We had worked with all three of these ships and had gotten to know some of their personnel. It was quite a sight when these destroyers limped into Tulagi Harbor, their bows completely blown off forward of their bridge area. Stub-nosed bulkheads just below the bridge were the most forward portion of each ship that remained visible. How they stayed afloat was a tribute to the resourcefulness of their officers and men. With help from the repair ship *Argonne,* each ship was "shored-up" as best as possible under the circumstances. This enabled each of them to make their way slowly across the Pacific in order to obtain major repairs and rebuilding so both could fight again.

On 23 October, I reported to Camp Crocodile for special orders for the *SC-761.* When I returned on board I announced that the ship would be departing for detailed maintenance at Noumea. It had been a long time since the bottom had been scraped and other routine maintenance performed. Our number had come up for this work so we must now depart. As a result we would not be able to take part in the upcoming invasion of Bougainville. Furthermore, once our maintenance was completed at Noumea, we would be assigned to operate out of Suva doing convoy work in the rear areas. Apparently, we had earned the right to have a period of easier duty. It would not be the R&R we longed for in Australia or New Zealand, but it would be a pleasant change. Other subchasers took up the burdens in the Solomons, and we would depart this area in two days.

Returning to our favorite buoy in Tulagi Harbor, we each eagerly looked forward to this change of duty.

CHAPTER 9

Suva Via Noumea

After topping off with fuel and water on early Sunday evening, 24 October, we remained overnight at the Tulagi water dock. Following breakfast the next morning, we got under way at 0730 for Noumea via Espiritu Santo. By 0745 we had cleared the submarine nets and bade farewell to Tulagi. With good weather and calm seas the *SC-761* proceeded alone to Espiritu Santo, where we stayed only overnight. Arriving late in the afternoon of 27 October, we took on fuel and water, and were under way early the next morning for Noumea. It was shortly after lunch on Sunday, 31 October, when we entered Noumea Harbor and moored to a buoy in Fisherman's Bay. Although it was Halloween, such a holiday meant nothing to us who were overseas, but the quartermaster made a reference to the holiday in the log book. Two-thirds of the crew were granted liberty, to expire at 2200.

Promptly the next morning, 1 November, I went ashore and reported in to ComSoPac for duty and for details pertaining to our routine maintenance. James T. Moore, coxswain, had borrowed a motor launch and carried Don Terry (Y1c), Randall Stevens Grimm (GM3c), and me ashore. Terry was to obtain the mail while Grimm was to check on the Antiaircraft Training Center, where we planned to send some personnel during our stay in Noumea. A staff car which had come to the landing carried me to headquarters. No sooner had I arrived there than a violent explosion shook the city. Smoke billowed up from the area known as the Nickel Dock. I knew Grimm was en route to that area to check on the availabilty of the schooling conducted by the above training center. I later learned he was near the Nickel Dock when the ammunition shipment exploded. He bravely entered the area, assisted in rescue operations and received burns and serious smoke inhalation. As a result he was transferred to the U.S. Navy Mobile Hospital Number Five for treatment. On the fifth he returned to the *SC-761* for duty, and I duly noted in his service record his bravery on this occasion.

None of our former personnel whom I have contacted can recall whether it was an ammunition barge or a dump of recently unloaded ammunition that exploded, but they do recall its violence. Moore has written that he had taken someone else ashore after Terry, Grimm and I had disembarked, and had just shoved off from the landing when the explosion erupted nearby. He wrote, "I distinctly remember our trip back to Noumea, because when that explosion happened I had just taken someone else ashore in a borrowed motor launch and was returning to our ship. There were plenty of fireworks going off and all I could do was give the motor launch full throttle and pray I would get back safely to the ship." This incident served to remind each of us the care that must always be exercised when handling ammunition.

At headquarters I learned the routine maintenance would be extensive and that we would be in Noumea approximately a month. I further learned we would be losing some very experienced petty officers. Among those were several who had been in the pre-commissioning detail: Chief Galford; Budzisz, SM1c; Grove, MoMM1c; and Singer, MoMM1c. They were transferred to the receiving station. Choinski, GM1c, who had come aboard at Miami, was transferred back to Gunners Mate School in Washington, D.C. In addition we lost West, BM2c and Hawkins, MoMM1c, both of whom had been with us since Miami. Others who came aboard now, or had done so earlier in the Solomons were: Zachry, F1c; Wilkens, F1c; Carpenter, F1c; King, MoMM2c; Womack, S1c(RM); Simpson, S1c(GM); Hammock, S2c; Haigwood, S2c; and Hess, S2c. Previously, I have mentioned that Netka, RM2c and McKnight, EM3c replaced Taraszka and Pullen. Now the composition of the crew was quite different from the one which existed when we had sailed from Balboa in February. Furthermore, Burrell, QM1c (soon to be a CQM) would now stand officer-of-the-deck watches in place of Chief Galford.

Among many other things, our time in Noumea included the task of scraping and wire brushing the bottom of the ship and painting it with special paints to prevent the rotting of the wooden hull. It was an all-hands involvement in dry dock over a period of days. Only Sansfacon, our cook, was spared this duty as he still had to prepare our meals and provide plenty of iced tea. Finally, all was accomplished by the end of November and I reported to ComSoPac that the ship was again ready for duty. During my visit with such staff I was advised that the *SC-761* was now attached to the Service Squadron, South Pacific Force, and would operate out of Suva in the Fiji Islands escorting primarily merchant ships.

On 5 December at 1200 we cast off our lines from the mooring buoy, stood down the channel and out to sea with the merchant ship, SS George Chaffey, following close astern. We were to escort it to the entrance of Suva Harbor, after which the *SC-761* would then proceed to Lautoka, a port in the western part of Viti Levu, the principal island in the Fijis. A day after rounding the southern edge of New Caledonia we began to encounter the heaviest seas we had ever experienced. The area between New Caledonia and the Fiji Islands is noted as a pathway for hurricanes.

It was late in the afternoon of the second day at sea when the sky became heavily overcast and rain soon developed. We secured all equipment both topside and below decks. Not long thereafter the winds reached gale force. A storm approaching hurricane status must have passed this vicinity earlier and we were in its edges. The waves seemed monstrous to us on that ship as the troughs between some waves were very deep. Convoy speed was sharply reduced, and we maneuvered so as to keep the sea forward of broad on the bow.

Many deck hands became seasick. The cook could only furnish sandwiches for those who wished to eat. To steer the ship under these conditions was a very tiring and exhausting job for the helmsman, so that watch was rotated every thirty minutes. A bucket was kept handy for any seasick helmsman with his relief standing by to assist him. The fact that we rode such stormy seas without any trouble is a tribute not only to the design of that modern subchaser but also to the exceptional skill of the craftsmen at Ipswich who had built our ship.

Later, in talking with the skipper of another subchaser, which had passed through this same storm escorting another merchant ship, I learned from him that the seas had been so heavy that some of the radio gear on his ship was wrenched from the bulkhead during a most violent wave action. Needless to say, we on the *SC-761* were most grateful for the calmer waters that occurred as we neared the Fijis.

Early on the morning of 9 December we sighted Viti Levu. By noon we had dropped off the Chaffey at the entrance to Suva Harbor and were backtracking towards Lautoka. During midafternoon we began to enter Navula Passage through the coral reefs that abound around much of Viti Levu and the Fiji Islands. Proceeding through the Nandi Waters, we passed Nakorokoro Point, passed along the west side of tiny Vio Island, circled around its northern tip staying south of Mbekana Island, and swung into the Lautoka Harbor area. By signal light we were directed to tie up to the one dock at this port, just astern of the SS *Lundys Lane* which we would next escort. This dock was the head of a tee with a very long stem which jutted out about 350 yards from the beach over coral and mud flats. We had safely made the trip and by now all traces of seasickness had evaporated.

Originally we were to be in Lautoka only overnight, but the next morning a hurricane warning delayed us. The port director advised us concerning the status of the hurricane. Late in the afternoon of the 10th, clouds were moving in and we were told to remain alert. Very early at dawn the next morning the wind was picking up, clouds were swirling in the sky, and we were directed to leave the dock. I chose to anchor in eleven fathoms of water to the leeward side of nearby Mbekana Island, an area with an excellent grey sand bottom. Using our best and heaviest anchor we put out thirty-two fathoms of chain. We had the smaller anchor rigged and prepared for any emergency. All hatches were battened down, and we awaited the arrival of the hurricane. Soon the heavy rain began, driven by the wind. The engine room was manned, and as the force of the wind increased we used the engines to ease the strain on the anchor chain. To make certain we were not dragging our anchor, we took frequent bearings on three objects ashore. Fortunately, the eye of the hurricane passed to the west of us, although we felt much of its force.

Once the huricane had fully passed our area, we were able to secure the engines. The quality of the design of our ship and its equipment, and the skill with which it had been constructed, were proven again by this successful encounter with a South Pacific hurricane.

Because of that storm our departure was delayed until the morning of 13 December; we returned to the dock. Under the circumstances the crew was able to have liberty at Lautoka. That town was the center of the sugar industry which was a major factor in the Fiji economy, and a large sugar mill was not far from the dock. Lautoka appeared to be a town of about 15,000 population, and we discovered a small, delightful hotel which had been used by some Australian tourists before the war. It had a bar that was still well-stocked from prewar days with several brands of fine scotch whiskey. Apparently not many devotees of that whiskey had passed this way since the outbreak of hostilities. Scotch was a rarity during the war, and totally absent from any officers' club in the South Pacific; we cherished this discovery. Except for the hurricane we spent a pleasant, relaxed three days at Lautoka.

The SS *Lundys Lane* having received its last cargo, we departed Lautoka with the *SC-761* for Espiritu Santo the morning of 13 December. Via Selwyn Strait we reached Espiritu Santo midafternoon the 15th. Again the seas were very rough because of the hurricane, causing much seasickness. We had rain most of the way until after we passed through Selwyn Strait, but the sea conditions were not as severe as those we had experienced out of Noumea. This trip was a quick turnaround as we departed Espiritu Santo on the 17th, escorting the SS *Stoney Point* and SS *Richmond* to Suva. Arriving in Suva Harbor shortly after dawn at 0645 on the 20th we had almost four days to become reacquainted with Suva. Needless to say, Jim Hannah and I quickly introduced Joe Effinger to the Grand Pacific Hotel. The same young native waiter, barefoot and in his customary immaculate white uniform, greeted us again with his impeccable "King's English." It had been nine months since Jim and I briefly visited the hotel, but he remembered us and our taste for fine scotch whiskey. We felt at home.

We lost our mascot, Feathers, while in the Fiji Islands. Whether it was at Lautoka or Suva, no one can now recollect. He often went ashore with some members of the crew and previously had always returned to the ship. Those two rough trips at sea may have convinced Feathers that shore duty was better. Or maybe he found a friendly female dog. We shall never know. The log of the *SC-761* does not reflect Feathers as being AWOL, but he was. Being a mutt, Feathers undoubtedly added some of his Heinz 57 lineage to the canine bloodlines in Viti Levu.

Early on Christmas Eve at 0555 we were under way escorting the SS *Joseph H. Priestley* to Lautoka. While at Lautoka over Christmas Eve, we tied up alongside a New Zealand ship, the SS *Kaikorai*, at the dock. We left the SS *Joseph H. Priestley* at Lautoka and were to depart on Christmas afternoon as the escort for the SS *Kaikorai*. When first notified of this trip we hoped we would go all the way to New Zealand, but to our dismay we learned that a New Zealand frigate would meet us at the halfway point to complete the escort duty.

Christmas Day was just another day, except that for lunch the cook prepared not Spam, but a baked ham! We had been out of the States for almost eleven months, and the crew had not worn a dress uniform since Miami. In fact, in the Solomons our dress had been very informal. Therefore, I suggested we all wear dress whites for about an hour, and I would get a crewman from the SS *Kaikorai* to take our group photograph. After lunch we shifted into Dress Whites, gathered about on the quarterdeck of our ship, and had our photograph taken. Then I took photographs of each division of the crew. Those photographs have been preserved all of these intervening years and are reproduced in this book. This was our only celebration for Christmas — much different from the one most of us had spent in Miami the previous year.

Following that picturetaking, we got under way, sailing out through the Nandi waters. The trip was uneventful, with relatively calm seas for a change. We met the New Zealand frigate about dusk on the 26th, and headed back to Suva. Arriving the morning of the 28th, we tied up at King's Wharf and remained there until our next duty on 2 January.

Accordingly, we were in port for New Year's Eve. Joe Effinger drew the duty that evening, so Jim Hannah and I in our dress-white uniforms attended a special dinner and festive party at the Grand Pacific Hotel. Various local officials and citizens were present, and it was a most pleasant evening. To Jim and I it made the war seem very far away. Two-thirds of the crew was on liberty, some had exchanged duty days, and therefore, most of those who wanted to celebrate went ashore for an evening of fun in various places.

January was a month of promotions. Jim Hannah and I were each promoted to lieutenant (junior grade) as of 1 January 1944. As commanding officer, I promoted Burrell to chief quartermaster, McMullen to MoMM1c, Groeschel to BM2c, McKnight to EM2c, Vandergriff to MoMM3c, and Carpenter, Wilkens and Zachry each to MoMM3c. As previously mentioned, Wootten was transferred back to the states for the officer V-12 program. Late December promotions included Moore to BM2c and Womack to RM3c. Earlier in October Terry had become Y1/c.

On 2 January we were under way to meet the *M. V. Matua*. Encountering her on the 3rd, we escorted the *Matua* back to Suva, and we tied up to King's Wharf. On the 8th we were advised of another approaching hurricane which was due to hit the Fijis the next day. Promptly, we moved to Naingalongado Harbor, the inner harbor for Suva, to seek refuge. This time we anchored in six fathoms of water in an area with a good gray mud bottom. We let out thirty fathoms of chain, again using our heaviest anchor. We prepared just as we had done earlier at Lautoka and waited. On this occasion winds of near hurricane force struck Suva just after midnight the 10th. At the height of the winds we again used our engines to ease the strain on the anchor, taking bearings as before. Once the storm passed over and the skies cleared, we hoisted anchor at 0855 on the 10th and moored alongside King's Wharf in this harbor.

On the 12th we escorted the SS *Esso Augusta* to Pago Pago, Samoa, but returned to Suva independently. On the 22nd we escorted the SS *Kincaid* to Espiritu Santo, bringing back the SS *John Sutter* on the 29th. As we tied up to King's Wharf on the 30th, Ens. Marson W. Pierce reported on board for duty as the new third officer.

Orders had not yet been received regarding Jim Hannah, Joe Effinger or me, but we knew they were imminent. As a matter of precaution we dispatched an inquiry to ComSoPac. Another era for the *SC-761* was about to begin.

The USS SC-761, under way, standing out of Espiritu Santo, Spring 1945. (A copy of Official U.S. Navy photograph that was in possession of former Lieutenant Elfelt, made prior to the original photo being slightly torn).

USS SC-761. On Liberty in Aukland. Left to right: Zachry, MoMM3c; Malone, SoM3c; Carpenter, MoMM3c.

USS SC-761

Gunnery drills at general quarters. In the South Pacific, Spring 1943. Left to right: Doscher (arm outstretched), Galford (trainer), Taraszka (loader), Choinski (pointer), West (foreground), Groeschel (standing background)

USS SC-761

Three members of the crew rinsing off with buckets of rainwater, after using the saltwater shower on the deck. En route to Bora Bora from Balboa, February 1943. Left to right: McMullen, Choinski, Budzisz.

The officers and crew of the USS SC-761 Christmas Day, 1943 at Lautoka, Fiji Islands.

1. Johnson, Matt, 1c
2. Simpson, S1c(GM)
3. McMullen, MoMM2c
4. Terry, Y1c
5. Sansfacon, SC!c
6. Haigwood, S2c
7. Hess, S2c
8. Carpenter, F1c
9. Grimm, GM3c
10. Ensign Hannah
11. Ensign Doscher
12. Ensign Effinger
13. Moore, BM2c
14. Groeschel, Coxwain

15. King, MoMM2c
16. Wootten, SoM2c
17. Bok, GM1c
18. Womack, S1c(RM)
19. Burrell, QM1c
20. Vandergriff, F1c
21. Waslousky, RM1c
22. McKnight, EM2c
23. Zachry, F1c
24. Wilkens, F1c
25. Hartmann, MoMM1c
26. Hammack, S2c
27. Netka, RM2c

The Australian/New Zealand coastwatchers returning to Guadalcanal from Bougainville on board the USS SC-761 26 July 1943. This photo was taken from the flying bridge of the SC-761. The coastwatchers gathered on the forecastle for this photo after they had taken a good hot shower, shaved, and eaten a good hot meal. They were in great spirits after their arduous experiences as coastwatchers in the jungles of Bougainville.

USS SC-761

Christmas Day, 1943. The Supply Division. Left to right: Hannah, Sansfacon, Johnson.

USS SC-761

Christmas Day, 1943. The Gunnery Division. Left to right: Grimm, Effinger, Bok, Simpson.

USS SC-761

Christmas Day, 1943. Front row (left to right): Waslousky, RM1c; McKnight, EM2c; Wotten, SoM2c. Back row: Netka, RM2c; Womack, S1c (RM).

USS SC-761
Left to right: Burrell; Terry, Y1c.

USS SC-761
Christmas Day, 1943. The Engineering Division. Front row (left to right): Wilkens, McMullen, Carpenter. Back row: King, Hartmann, Zachry.

USS SC-761

Christmas Day, 1943. The Deck Division. Front row (left to right): Moore, Simpson, Hess. Back row: Hammack, Groeschel, Haigwood, Vandergriff.

The USS SC-761 *at anchor in Purvis Bay, Florida Islands, Solomons, April 1943. This is in the time when Purvis Bay was mostly deserted except for an occasional subchaser.*

Ensign Doscher, Ensign Hannah, and Lieutenant Balcom at Purvis Bay, Florida Island (in the Solomon Islands), April 1943. These are the three officers who sailed the USS SC-761 from Miami to the Solomon Islands.

Reunion at the Everglades Club, Palm Beach, March 1990. Henry Doscher, Ronald Balcom, and James Hannah. These are the three officers who sailed the USS SC-761 from Miami to the Solomon Islands.

The native chief on Ugi Island, with his relatives and retinue, along with two junior officers of the USS LST 460. The USS SC-761 had escorted that LST into Selwyn Bay, Ugi Island, on 13 July 1943. Photograph taken 14 July.

Lieutenant Balcom, preparing his uniforms for his departure to the States from the Solomon Islands. September 1943. USS SC-761.

Ensign Doscher, while commanding officer, USS SC-761, October 1943, in the Solomon Islands.

Ensign Hannah, while executive officer, USS SC-761, October 1943, in the Solomon Islands. One of his additional duties at that time was navigator.

Ensign Effinger at the signal light on the flying bridge of the USS SC-761. In the Solomon Islands, October 1943. He was the newly arrived third officer, and he was then communications officer, among other duties.

Ensign Pierce, third officer; Lieutenant Hannah, commanding officer; Ensign Effinger, executive officer. On the lawn of the Grand Pacific Hotel, Suva, March 1944.

USS SC-761
Moore, Coxwain, on liberty in the Fiji Islands, April 1944.

USS SC-761
On liberty in the Fiji Islands, April 1944. Left to right: Bok, Sansfacon, Wilkens, Groeschel.

USS SC-761

Gunnery drills at general quarters. In the South Pacific, Spring 1943. Left to right: Johnson, Bok, Terry, Sansfacon.

At Bora Bora, early March 1943. Standing (left to right): Ensign Hannah and Lieutenant Balcom. Kneeling: Ensign Doscher and Chief Galford with mascot, Feathers.

The USS SC-761 at anchor, Bora, Bora, March 1943. After the long trip from
Balboa. (note some stlks of bananas hanging on the flying bridge.)

Photo taken about January 1945 (or Fall 1944?). Left to right: Hartmann,
CMoMM; Slucher; Mars; Zachry; Grimm.

Ensign Effinger, third officer; Ensign Hannah, X.O. USS SC-761 *in the Solomon Islands, October 1943.*

The officers of USS SC-761, *Christmas Day, 1943. Ensign Hannah, X.O.; Ensign Doscher, C.O.; Ensign Effinger, third officer.*

Lt. Warner Keeley, Jr., commanding officer of USS SC-641, with natives on San Cristobal Island. September 1943.

The USS SC-761 hoisting anchor at Bora Bora, March 1943, in preparation for departure to Pago Pago, 15 March 1943.

CHAPTER 10

Suva, Taveuni and Tongatapu

In the morning mail of 4 February 1944, the appropriate orders were received to effect the change of command. Pursuant to ComSoPac order P16-4/00/(60), serial 662p, dated 14 January 1944, I was to be transferred to SCTC at Miami for advanced training when relieved by Jim Hannah. He and I promptly began a meticulous inventory and report of all the confidential and secret publications on hand. I had to prepare and sign fitness reports for both Hannah and Effinger, the general mess inventory had to be calculated, and the appropriate letter reports readied for the Chief of Naval Operations and for the Commander Naval Bases, Fiji. All of this being accomplished that same day, formal change of command would occur the next morning.

On 5 February at 0800, with the crew at quarters on the quarterdeck, Jim Hannah and I each read our orders. Exchanging salutes, he properly relieved me as commanding officer. Thereupon, after shaking hands and having a personal word with each member of ship's company, I departed the *SC-761* which had been my home and my life for thirteen months.

I then reported to the Commander Naval Bases, Fiji for transportation to the States and for temporary billeting in the officer's quarters. I was authorized air travel, Class Four priority, so I had to wait at Suva for several days for space on the former Pan Am seaplanes. In the meantime I relaxed and even played a game of golf at the local British Country Club. That was an interesting experience; golf balls were scarce and cost one dollar, but native caddies were only five cents! Because there were no water holes as traps, and the natives never lost sight of where a ball landed, even when in the rough, only one golf ball was necessary each round.

75

On 10 February Class Four airplane space became available. The Pan Am seaplane landed in Suva Harbor. A launch took me to the plane, and soon we were airborne. Circling over the harbor as we took off, I had one final glimpse of the *SC-761* moored to King's Wharf. It was an emotional experience as I was leaving behind men I had come to admire and respect. They were dedicated and responsible persons with qualities as good as you can find. After a few months on a small ship everyone gets to know each other—learning of their families, their hopes, and their aspirations. Some would stay in touch and be my friends to this day. In such a departure one does not merely say "goodbye"; rather, one says *"au revoir"* or perhaps *"auf Wiedersehen,"* which may better express a temporary parting.

Through extensive interviews with surviving members of former ship's company, combined with a review of official records, I have been able to piece together the remaining story of the *SC-761*.

Lt. (jg) James B. Hannah was the commanding officer, while Ens. Joseph F. Effinger was executive officer. The newly arrived Ens. Marson W. Pierce became the third officer. After my departure, the ship entered the local Marine Railway for scraping and painting, as well as for caulking the deck, sides, and bottom. Much of that work was accomplished by native workmen, but ship's company was responsible for the painting. In the midst of this, James Moore had to be temporarily transferred to the local naval dispensary for an appendectomy. Since subchasers have no medical personnel, the *SC-761* was fortunate that few men became ill and needed a physician. In the Solomon Islands we had two or three men go to a naval dispensary for a few days with tropical skin rashes. Even Jim Hannah entered the naval dispensary at Suva for three days in May because of illness. Otherwise, the crew was remarkably healthy.

Generally the same type of convoy duty was continued during the time Jim Hannah was skipper. However, two noteworthy missions occurred while he was in command. In the first instance, the natives on the island of Taveuni, an island in the Fijis, just southeast of Vanua Levu, reported that a loose mine had drifted into one of their bays and was a danger to them. As a result, commander naval bases, Fiji sent F. D. O'Brien BM2c, a mine disposal expert, aboard the *SC-761* and ordered the *SC-761* to proceed to Taveuni to disarm or destroy the floating mine. The *SC-761* set sail for Taveuni. Taveuni had no harbor and in those days generally only native craft visited the island. Naval ships had no reason to go there, and charts were somewhat inadequate and outdated. What Hydrographic Office charts that did exist were copied from a British admiralty chart based upon surveys between 1878 and 1880. Thus the *SC-761* had to proceed with caution as it approached the southeastern area of Taveuni, where the mine had drifted into a cove near Vurevure Bay.

Taveuni is a long, thin island with a mountain ridge down its center like a spinal backbone. Those ridges rise about 4,000 feet and are densely covered with jungle. There were coconut plantations in the flat areas near the coastlines. Coral reefs were a distinct danger for ships traversing that area.

By 1200 on 4 April, the ship approached the eastern area of Taveuni along its south coast, opposite the tiny island then called Nggamea. Special lookouts as well as special sea detail were posted. A leadsman was on the forecastle and soundings were being taken with the fathometer. Soon natives were observed on the shoreline making motions to indicate the best course of travel for the ship to enable it to safely approach Vurevure Bay. While the ship was carefully nearing the beach area after entering the bay, a native chief swam out and came aboard the *SC-761* to act as a pilot. Thanks to the British colonial education system, the natives spoke some English. With his help, the *SC-761* was piloted to a safe anchorage in Vurevure Bay. After the crew dropped the starboard anchor at the place designated by the chief, the ship remained some distance from the beach.

O'Brien was introduced to the native chief as the navy's munitions expert who would disarm the troublesome mine. After some discussion, it was decided that O'Brien, Effinger, and Burrell would go ashore to handle the mine problem. Effinger strapped on his sidearms, and the three clambered over the side and into the ship's wherry. It was soon stranded on a sandbar. The chief had three men swim out to assist O'Brien, Burrell, and Effinger. Placing them on their shoulders, the natives carried the landing party ashore. After being led to the nearby cove in which the mine was floating, O'Brien had to wade in waist-deep water to reach the mine. It was very late in the afternoon before the mine was disarmed, but O'Brien accomplished his chore with skill.

The natives were so grateful that the chief invited the ship's officers and crew for dinner, dancing, and entertainment. Because the ship had to remain overnight, the invitation was accepted. Jim Hannah and a skeleton crew remained aboard the ship; everyone else went ashore for the festivities. The ship's wherry was used in shifts partway, but the crew had to wade in knee-deep water the final stretch to the beach. When they reached the area of the grass huts, all navy personnel were requested to remove their wet clothing and shoes. Each was given a knee-length sarong to wear so they would be dressed the same as the natives. The uniform of the evening ashore on Taveuni was a colorful sarong and bare feet!

The passengers of the *SC-761* were greeted with throbbing music made by natives beating on various-sized hollow logs. A native drink was available in copious quantities, with coconuts used as glasses. The dinner, consisting of various native dishes, was prepared by native girls. After an extensive cocktail hour, dinner was served in a large hut with a dirt floor. The table was a reed mat placed on the floor. Yet in this very primitive and remote area, there was a place-setting of silver, properly arranged, for each guest. How and where the chief had accumulated that silver is unknown. However, there was no china to go with the silver, only crude wooden bowls from which to eat. It was even a greater surprise to Ensign Effinger when one of the young ladies placed a bottle of Lea & Perrins sauce on the table in front of him.

Upon inquiry, he learned that this island, like several others, was owned by Lever Bros., which ran the coconut plantations harvested by the natives. This London company had sent its British manager of these island plantations several cases of sauce at his request so he could season his food. In turn, the manager had given several bottles to the chief of Taveuni Island.

The party lasted very late with much food, drink, and dancing. Bacchus reigned supreme on Taveuni that night as the men of the *SC-761* wholeheartedly joined in the native festivities. It was a totally unexpected but very welcomed occasion of revelry and frivolity, a relief from the tensions of wartime duty, thoroughly enjoyed by the men of the *SC-761*.

Perhaps no other navy ship experienced a similar event. Such festivity was possible only because the *SC-761* had such a small crew and this was a remote island, apparently never previously visited by any military or any tourist. One former crewman wrote:

> Two of us spent the night with a family that had two teenage daughters. We were invited to spend the night. The girls slept on palm leaf mats on the dirt floor of the family hut. However, we each had a bed made from palm tree logs, covered with woven palm leaves. Unfortunately their father, a big, husky native, slept on the floor between us and his daughters. Each time we rose up to look at the girls, Papa would also rise up. We soon got the message, gave up and went to sleep.

The next morning the guests from the *SC-761* were given a breakfast of grilled fresh fish and some white root that the natives used for bread. Breakfast was eaten with one's fingers. As was their custom, the men ate first then the women ate. After fond farewells, it was time to return to duty. By 1000 the party group had returned aboard ship, swimming much of the way. The crew thoroughly enjoyed the fine hospitality afforded them by those grateful natives. This mine disposal mission was a very memorable experience for the men of the *SC-761*. Each former member of ship's company with whom I contacted has a fond recollection of this sojourn to the remote and primitive Fijian island of Taveuni.

At 1045 anchor was hoisted and the ship got under way, carefully departing Vurevure Bay at a very slow speed. Early the following morning the *SC-761* arrived at Suva and tied up to King's Wharf at 0710. F. D. O'Brien left the ship and the *SC-761* was once again ready for the convoy routine.

After several convoy trips, during some of which extremely rough seas were encountered and celestial navigation was impeded by overcast skies, the second memorable event of Jim Hannah's command occurred. The ship received notice it would escort the *M. V. Matua* to the island of Tongatapu, the main island in the group known as the Tonga Islands. Located to the southeast of the Fiji Islands, the Tongas were renowned throughout the ships of the South Pacific Fleet. Scuttlebutt concerned the sexual prowess and proclivity of its native girls of Polynesian ancestry. Having heard many sea stories about the Tongas, the crew looked forward to this assignment. At 2340 on 8 May the *SC-761* pulled away from King's Wharf and stood out to sea with the *M. V. Matua* following astern.

With calm seas, under beautiful skies, it was an easy convoy trip. As the ships neared Nukualola, the principal town located in the broad bay on the north side of Tongatapu, the *SC-761* was directed by signal light to tie up to Yellow Pier. At 1143 it was moored alongside that pier. The *SC-640* was in port from another convoy but was anchored in the bay rather than being at the dock. In short order, the reason became apparent. Jim Hannah reports that after about three hours various young Polynesian females, clad in sarongs, appeared on the public dock. They were continually climbing aboard, taunting the crew, who reluctantly were attempting to remove the native girls from the ship. The port director saw what was happening and directed the ship to leave the dock and moor alongside the *SC-640*. This accomplished at 1742, the crew then had their evening meal, and those young females were the topic of conversation. As the sun set, some of the girls swam out to the ship. One told the crew she would like to dance on the deck and even in the wardroom. Jim

Hannah says he received many sad glances when her request to climb aboard and dance was firmly denied.

Nevertheless, girls did swim out to the two subchasers during the night and easily enticed some of the off-duty crew to jump into the water and swim ashore. Later, sea stories, probably somewhat embellished, confirmed the rumors the crew of the SC-761 had heard about Tonga. One member of the crew, whose name will remain anonymous, boasted that during the night he had married an island princess in a native ceremony. Regrettably for some, the next day before noon the ship was under way alone for Suva. Now the crew could say it had experienced Tonga and would like to return.

No sooner had the ship arrived in Suva than it was advised that its port of operations would be Espiritu Santo in the New Hebrides. On 16 May it departed Suva for the last time, sailing alone. It had three passengers and thirty-two sacks of mail destined for Espiritu Santo. During those last three months in Suva, there had been some crew changes. Don Terry, the yeoman, had been transferred on 9 March, while two sonarmen were received: R. J. Malone and R. A. Miklos. Other transfers to and from the ship occurred regularly thereafter and were too numerous to specify here.

The faithful and very capable mess attendant, Julius Plato (Willie) Johnson, has not been mentioned regarding promotion. This young black man was most intelligent, and on his own initiative, helped by fellow crewmen, learned the Morse Code. He became extremely proficient in using the blinker light, and acted as a signalman on some watches. He studied the book for third class signalman and passed the test with flying colors. During his tour of duty on the SC-761 three separate commanding officers recommended that he be cross-rated to signalman, third class. Such a request had been pending with the Bureau Of Naval Personnel for some time, so any change in rating was delayed awaiting results. Each request was denied ultimately. Before President Truman issued his famous executive order in 1948, the armed forces of the United States were strictly segregated and ratings were restricted. Willie's own shipmates knew of his capabilities, but the system at that time did not permit the recommendations from his commanding officers to be honored.

After Willie was discharged, he graduated from college in Texas, became a public school teacher, and was principal of a high school in East Texas during the last few years before his retirement. His abilities and his keen mind were borne out during his civilian career after World War II.

During this trip to Espiritu Santo, a small vibration occurred in one of the propellers. Upon arrival at Espiritu Santo, the commanding officer requested a check of the propellers in a dry dock. When space became available on 23 May the *SC-761* entered the ARD-5, the local dry dock. A thorough check revealed that the starboard screw must be replaced. This replacement was completed the morning of 31 May. Again the *SC-761* was ready for duty and tied up alongside the USS *Mindanao*.

On 1 June 1944, a motor launch came alongside carrying Ens. John O'Brien Elfelt. To the great delight of Jim Hannah, Ensign Elfelt reported on board as the new third officer. As in the past, orders were received whereby Lieutenant (jg) Hannah was to be relieved by newly promoted Lieutenant (jg) Effinger as commanding officer, with Ensign Pierce to be the new executive officer. Feverishly working on the appropriate paperwork, they had all in order by noon. With the crew at quarters, at 1200 on 1 June, the fifth commanding officer of the ship took charge and assumed responsibility. Jim Hannah promptly departed the ship and went ashore to arrange transportation back to the States. Soon he would resume the honeymoon that had been interrupted at Miami. Later he reported to the SCTC at Miami for advanced training.

CHAPTER 11

Espiritu Santo and New Zealand

Rather than being assigned convoy duty, the *SC-761* became a station ship at Espiritu Santo, patrolling the harbor entrances as a precaution against possible enemy submarines and escorting merchant ships through the mine fields. This usually involved three days of patrolling either Segound Channel, Coolidge Passage, Scarff Channel, Diamond Passage, or Undine Passage. The duty was rotated among the several subchasers now at Espiritu Santo. Following the completion of a patrol, a subchaser had three days in port. On some off-duty days they had antisubmarine practice with the USS *S-38*. At other times they fired the mousetraps and the K-guns with depth charges to be certain such equipment was in good working order. Only once during the next few months was a possible submarine reported in the area. That was on 14 June 1944 and the *SC-761*, joined by the *SC-729*, made a detailed sonar search off of Tutuba Island. No enemy submarine was found, and the ships returned to port late that evening.

On 20 June Chief Burrell, who had been with the ship since Tompkinsville, was transferred back to the States, where he became a navigation instructor. Since Chief Burrell had been standing watch as an officer-of-the-deck, the skipper selected Leon Netka, recently promoted to RM1c, to take his place for that duty. This arrangement had been standard procedure ever since the ship left Miami, as it made available three people who could fill such billet under the three-section watch assignments. Accordingly, the skipper could obtain some rest and be available for call during any watch section.

Starting in July, members of the crew began to attend various gunnery, radar, and aircraft recognition schools ashore. This was rotated among the crew so that over a period of time each man attended at least the gunnery and aircraft recognition schools. Those who stood any watches on the bridge attended the radar schools. This was excellent training, especially for those who had recently come aboard, and it was a good refresher for the others.

In October the ship was notified it would be sent to Aukland, New Zealand, for a short period of rest and recreation, popularly known in the fleet as R&R. It had been a long time coming. All of. the major elements of the fleet in this area occasionally sailed to New Zealand or Australia for R&R, but somehow the subchasers had been overlooked. The *SC-761* had no complaint, as the prior recent duty operating out of Suva had been a pleasant interlude. But now they were ready to go to New Zealand.

Early on 9 October the *SC-761* was under way for Aukland, accompanied by two other subchasers, one of which was the its sister ship, the *SC-760*. On the way to Auckland they had very favorable weather and everyone was in an excited mood. On 14 October at 2210 the lookout reported Cape Brett Light in sight. It was a joyful moment and all hands came topside to witness this sighting. Very early on the 15th the three subchasers entered Watamata Harbor at Aukland. The *SC-761* was directed to tie up at Prince's Wharf, while the accompanying two subchasers were directed to another area of the port to join other subchasers. This separation of ships would turn out to be fortuitous for the *SC-761* before this sojourn was finished.

Now began ten glorious days of R&R. With four watch sections, three-fourths of the crew could have liberty at any one time. In my recent talks with Leon Netka, RM1c, he told me that the crew of the *SC-761* rented a floor of a small hotel, the Jolly Mont, for those ten days. It became the base of operations for our crew on liberty. Netka relates that the owners of this hotel often had naval personnel stay with them during R&R, and as one of the amenities they served breakfast in bed. It was gratis and a real treat.

Joe Effinger and Marson (Bub) Pierce each report to me that everyone on the ship had a 4.0 good time in Auckland. Friendly female companionship was enjoyed, true to the old refrain: "When I'm not near the girl I love, I love the girl I'm near." Joe Effinger tells me that a couple of his crew tried to get him to sail out into the ocean and perform a marriage ceremony for them with their ladies of the evening. Of course he declined. Time away from home and from female companionship undoubtedly muddled their thinking. Some made trips into the countryside to see parts of New Zealand; others visited in the homes of New Zealanders. It was a pleasure to relax away from the strains of duty. Even little things as insignificant as fresh milk were appreciated.

About the third day the subchasers were in port, all commanding officers were summoned to a meeting with the base commander. They received a blistering lecture about the flagrant violations of security rules being exhibited by the subchaser fleet. Apparently the crews of one or more subchasers at the other pier, where several SCs were tied up, had invited girls to spend the night aboard. Joe Effinger pointed out that the SC-761 was in another area of the harbor and could not be involved in the infractions reported by the shore patrol at the other location. Joe was excused from the meeting and saved from the reprimands incurred by others. Thus, it was fortunate the SC-761 was at a different dock in another area of the harbor. Also, the crew of the SC-761 had been very wise to rent the floor of the Jolly Mont Hotel as its base of operations.

Those glorious ten days ended all too soon. On 26 October the ship stood out of the harbor traveling alone. Maybe because of the above incident involving some of the other subchasers, those which had accompanied the SC-761 from Espiritu Santo departed earlier. Joe Effinger reported that early in the evening of the second day out from Auckland, the SC-761 received a coded radio message on the Fox Schedule as follows:

> You are on a collision course with an American merchant vessel X
> Expect to make contact at midnight X.

This contact time was some three hours or so away, and, in addition the matter must have been determined earlier in order for it to be encoded and transmitted on the fox schedules. In spite of questions in his mind, skipper Joe Effinger was on the flying bridge that entire evening. He wrote: "Sure enough, at precisely the scheduled hour we sighted that vessel. After an exchange of I.D.s we proceeded as ordered. Can you imagine? Here we were in the middle of the South Pacific and somewhere, somebody was directing traffic so exactly!" What an excellent example of proficiency in the naval command then monitoring such ocean traffic, particularly when one realizes its importance with all vessels sailing under very strict darkened ship conditions.

Some bad weather prevented precise starsight navigation. Joe reports his dead reckoning navigation skills were shaken when the ship made landfall with an en route island at the scheduled time, but the island appeared on the wrong side of the ship. Fortunately, the clouds parted and the sun shone bright and clear just about noon.

Quickly he took a LAN sight with the sextant and the latitude confirmed that he had the correct island; they were just on the wrong side of it! A slight course adjustment steered the ship safely to Espiritu Santo. They arrived on Halloween, just as in the previous year we had arrived at Noumea on that same holiday. The past year had gone by in a hurry.

While at Espiritu Santo, Hartmann and Sansfacon each were advanced to chief officer and were transferred. Many other transfers occurred so that by 1 January 1945, of the crew which had sailed from Balboa, only Johnson, cook, third class, was left on board. Later, about the time of V-E Day, he would be transferred.

On 16 December Ens. James T. Maddox reported on board for duty as the new third officer. The same routine of change of command took place. Lieutenant (jg) Pierce became commanding officer, and Ens. John O'B. Elfelt advanced to executive officer. Joe Effinger went back to SCTC at Miami. The rest of December 1944 and the first four months of 1945 were spent on screening duty at Espiritu Santo. Christmas was just another day, although the ship got to go out of the harbor to practice shooting at a target towed behind an airplane. During the early spring of 1945 the Navy took an official photograph of the *SC-761*, apparently for publicity purposes. It is a fine shot of the ship, under way through the waters of a portion of Espiritu Santo Harbor, with Lieutenant (jg) Pierce on the flying bridge. In my research for this book I could only uncover a slightly torn copy of such official photo. It is reproduced herein and to me is one of the better photographs of a World War II-vintage subchaser while under way.

In May the *SC-761* went to Noumea for generator repair and routine overhaul. Noumea was now a much quieter military place — no longer a bustling headquarters of activity. The war had moved so far north, Noumea was now in the extreme rear area. While repairs were in progress, Lieutenant Kavalar reported aboard to assume command. A full lieutenant taking command of a subchaser at this stage of the war! This was confusing as well as contrary to the procedure within the subchaser fleet. Marson Pierce, the skipper, fired off an inquiry to BuPers. A month later while at Guam, it was determined that BuPers or SCTC had mistakenly typed "SC-761" on Lieutenant Kavalar's orders, when in fact he was to supposed to assume command of the "PC-761" in the Aleutians. This error allowed the *SC-761* to have four officers on board for a month, when there was bunk space for only three. Sleeping was done in shifts.

Once the repairs were completed in Noumea, there was no reason to send the *SC-761* back to Espiritu Santo which was now far removed from the war areas. The Marshalls, Guam, Saipan, and Tinian and other Central Pacific invasions had all occurred during 1944. Luzon was being liberated in the spring of 1945. Iwo Jima and Okinawa were invaded in the spring of 1945 as the Allied forces approached the Japanese home islands. Therefore, the *SC-761* obtained a new duty station in Guam in the Central Pacific area. The ship would travel there by way of Guadalcanal and Eniwetok.

The last wartime duty of the *SC-761* and its crew was at hand.

CHAPTER 12

Eniwetok, Guam and San Francisco

Early on 12 June 1945, at 0640 the *SC-761* was under way for Guadalcanal and Tulagi. Standing alone out of the harbor of Noumea, it soon passed Maitre Island Light to starboard and Amidee Light to port. Since it did not stop at Espiritu Santo, the ship arrived off Lunga Point, Guadalcanal, the late afternoon of 16 June. Anchoring there overnight, it proceeded to Tulagi Harbor the next morning to replenish fuel and water. Entering Tulagi it tied up at Pier 6. What a change at Tulagi from the conditions which existed in April 1943. Tulagi now had at least six piers and all types of extensive facilities for the fleet. Perhaps even USO Shows had come that way, while in 1943 those shows never ventured farther north than Espiritu Santo.

The *SC-761* was advised that it was to escort some LSMs to Guam via Eniwetok. Accordingly the morning of 20 June, the *SC-761* was under way to Eniwetok escorting the *LSM*s 2, 15, 85, 162, and 246. Convoy speed was only 9 knots. This was an uneventful trip with favorable weather, and the convoy arrived at Eniwetok Harbor on 26 June. The *SC-761* moored alongside the *SC-633* and late the next afternoon took on fuel and water. The morning of 28 June, the *SC-761* stood out of the harbor, escorting the same LSMs, en route to Guam. On 3 July, this little convoy arrived at Apra Harbor, Guam, and the *SC-761* tied up alongside the *SC-716*. Quite a few other subchasers were in Apra Harbor, notably the *SCs 658, 677, 669, 1041, 1275, 1317,* and *1325.* All were being used for screening duty of Apra Harbor.

Promptly upon arrival at Guam, Lieutenant Kavalar received his corrected orders and he departed for the Aleutian Islands. Just three days later, Ens. Floyd T. Gates reported on board the *SC-761* to be its new third officer. As in the past, similar orders were received detaching Lieutenant Pierce as commanding officer, designating now Lieutenant Elfelt as the new commanding officer and Ensign Maddox as executive officer. Following the same routine, Lieutenant Pierce departed for advanced training at SCTC.

During the rest of the month of July and much of August, the *SC-761* had patrol duty, screening for enemy submarines off Apra Harbor. Ensign Gates suffered severely from fungus infections incurred in the tropics and from some acid burns. He was transferred to the base hospital at Guam. The ship's log does not reflect the circumstances whereby he acquired such burns, but they were so severe he could not return to duty. In his place on 25 August, the commander at Guam sent Ens. Warren A. Miller to be the new third officer.

At this time, "the bomb" was dropped on Japan, and the war ended with the same suddenness with which it had begun. Everyone sensed that they would soon be home. Congress urged speedy demobilization. Now the major objective was to send ships back to the States and bring people home. Soon the *SC-761* was one of a group of subchasers which started the long journey home. On 14 September Ensign Gates reported back on board as a passenger since apparently he would need very special treatment in naval medical facilities in the States.

On the morning of 15 September, the *SC-761* was under way, standing out of Apra Harbor, in company with the *SCs 677, 699, 1041, 1275,* and *1325* en route to Eniwetok. All ships now used their running lights. How great it was to travel with lights! Now standing watch was much easier. Everyone was in a great mood. We had won the war and it was time to go home! The feeling was the same throughout the fleet.

On 20 September, these ships reached Eniwetok, took on fuel and water, and were under way for Johnston Island early the next morning. For some reason *SC-677* was left behind. Passing Eluk Island on the 23rd, they didn't arrive at Johnston Island until 28 September.

After taking on fuel and water, these five subchasers quickly departed for Pearl Harbor the morning of 29 September; they arrived three days later. The ships remained in Pearl Harbor for some twelve days. The authorities there carefully reviewed the rosters of these ships to ascertain which men had significant duty time remaing under their enlistment contracts. Due to the pressure from Congress, demobilization created problems for the navy who attempted to keep the fleet properly manned. After review, seven men were transferred to the receiving station, and seven due for discharge were sent aboard as replacements so as to return them to the States.

Finally, on 14 October, the *SC-761* departed Pearl Harbor for San Francisco in company with the *LST 1139*, and the *SCs 514, 631, 669, 733, 990, 991, 1041, 1048, 1270, 1317, 1319, 1325*, and *1374*. The next day, on orders from ComSerPac, the subchasers dropped all depth charges, flares, cartridges, and rockets.

Late on the evening of 24 October, at 2215, the lookout on the *SC-761* spotted Farallon Light. San Francisco was ahead! This sighting caused all hands to come topside in order to witness this glimpse of America. It was a time of rejoicing. Most of the crew stayed on deck throughout the night. It was difficult to sleep amid all the excitement of arriving in the United States.

At 0550 an 25 October, the convoy began to enter San Franciso Channel. By signal light the *SC-761* was directed to the ammunition pier at Mare Island Navy Yard. Docking there at 1340, the crew quickly unloaded all amunition. The ship was then directed to Treasure Island and told to moor at Pier 16. It tied up there at 1445, and Ensign Gates was transferred to the naval hospital on Treasure Island. The preliminary transfer of equipment and supplies began to take place.

On 29 October, all men due for immediate discharge were transferred to the receiving station, with only a handful left on board. Ensign Maddox was transferred for further assigment since he did not have enough points for separation from active duty. Of the men who had served under me during my command in the South Pacific, only George Henry Haigwood, now GM2c, was aboard at the end. Haigwood had come aboard the *SC-761* at Noumea in November 1943 as a fresh S2c, he soon became a gunner's mate striker. To his credit, he made second class during the intervening two years.

Before mid-November the ship moved to the Mare Island Navy Yard for removal of armament and other special navy equipment. With that accomplished it was now time for the formal act of decommissioning. There was no "spit and polish" ceremony as had occurred at its commissioning at Ipswich in September 1942. Rather, an inspecting officer from the navy yard came aboard on 28 November and checked into matters with Lieutenant (jg) Elfelt, the final commanding officer. With all in order, the national ensign and the union jack were lowered, the commission pennant was hauled down from the truck of the mast, and the final entries were made in the log of the USS *SC-761*. As his final official act, Commanding Officer John Elfelt signed the log book in accordance with naval regulations. He and the rest of the crew thereupon departed the ship.

The saga of this little fighting ship was at an end. While the *SC-761* had entered the fleet in the fall of 1942 enlivened by the vim, vigor and the high spirits of its crew, dedicated to doing its best to help win the war, in the hectic rush of demobilization in the fall of 1945 following total victory, its career ended in something of a wimper. Like many other ships in the Splinter Fleet it had performed its duties admirably and in some small measure had contibuted to the victorious result.

The saga of the *SC-761* is, in a sense, the story of the Splinter Fleet, a microcosm of that unsung portion of the United States Navy.

Epilogue

Each of the former commanding officers returned to Miami and the SCTC for advanced training, except Marson Pierce and John Elfelt. These two would have done likewise except for the fact that the war ended suddenly. Upon returning stateside, Pierce was on his thirty days of leave when "the bomb" was dropped on Japan, so he was promptly released to inactive duty. For a short time he worked for General Electric, then ended up ranching in Colorado. He is now retired, and he and his wife reside in Gunnison, Colorado.

The final commanding officer was John Elfelt. Not long after separation from active duty, he went back to New Zealand for six months, then returned to Anoka, Minnesota, where he is now in the real estate business. He and his wife have seven sons, the eldest of whom graduated second in his class at the U.S. Naval Academy.

After finishing advanced training at SCTC, Ronald B. Balcom became executive officer of the USS *Robert Paine (DE 576)*. Thereafter he failed a hearing test in a physical examination and became convoy control officer in the port director's office in New York Harbor. Shortly after the war ended, he was released to inactive duty and returned to his investment business. Besides a summer home on Fishers Island, New York, a chalet at Klosters and a town house at Vail, he and his wife, Lou, have a lovely home on Island Drive in Palm Beach. In the spring of 1990 they invited Jim Hannah, his wife Rosemary, and me to their Palm Beach home for a mini-reunion, followed by a dinner party at the Everglades Club. A photograph of Ronnie, Jim, and me taken at that reunion appears in this book and should be contrasted with the photograph of the three of us taken beside the native hut in the Solomons in 1943.

From SCTC Jim Hannah went to gunnery school at Washing-

91

ton, D.C., then to the USS *William Seiverling (DE 441)*, where he became gunnery and torpedo officer. That ship was the flagship of Destroyer Escort Divison #70, operating between Ulithi and Japan. It sailed to Tokyo Bay and took part in the surrender. Screening the harbor entrance during the surrender proceedings, it then entered port and dropped anchor near the USS *Missouri*. Following his release from active duty, Jim entered Harvard Law School. Upon graduation, he returned to Minneapolis and joined the law firm of Mackall, Crounse and Moore, from which he retired as a partner in 1989. He and Rosemary have two children. On two recent occasions I have joined them, their children, and their grandchildren for winter vacations in Florida.

Completing his advanced training, Joe Effinger drew the plum of an assignment — commanding officer of the USS *PC-566*, which was the school ship for SCTC. Therefore, he spent the rest of the war in Miami. After release to inactive duty, he returned to General Electric, ultimately retiring as an executive in its Sales Division. He and his wife reside in Plantation, Florida, a suburb of Fort Lauder-dale where he plays golf each day.

Following his transfer from the *SC-761*, Chief Quartermaster George A. Burrell was assigned to the U.S. Naval Training Center at Sampson, New York. At that duty station he was the instructor of celestial navigation and head of the quartermaster school until the Japanese surrendered. He remained on active duty until 2 March 1946, first in the port director's office at Battery Park, New York, then in the Lido Beach Separation Center as legal advisor to those being discharged. After his discharge, he resumed the practice of law in New York City, ultimately becoming a partner in the Park Avenue firm of Kelley, Drye & Warren. Besides a summer place on Nassau Point, Cutchogue, Long Island, New York, he makes his home at Jensen Beach, Florida. George and his late wife, Ione, only recently deceased, have two daughters and one grandson. To this day George is an avid yachtsman and tennis player.

Don Terry, our yeoman, married Margaret upon his return stateside. She was from a family in Miami, so following his discharge from the navy, Don became a public schoolteacher in the Miami school system. He retired from that job several years ago; he and Margaret made Miami their home until his recent death. In 1990 and again in 1991, they hosted a mini-reunion of Joe Effinger, Jim Hannah, George Burrell and me, along with Rosemary Hannah and Ione Burrell.

James T. Moore, who a became BM2/c on the *SC-761*, returned to Miami and became a member of ship's company at SCTC. He had duty as master-at-arms along with that of shore patrol. Discharged in October 1945, he returned to Lynchburg, Virginia. There he began a career first with Greyhound, then with the Trailways bus system. He retired as purchasing agent several years ago and still resides in Lynchburg.

Julius Plato Johnson, who was first a mess attendant and later a cook, originally came from Cameron, Texas, joining the navy at age seventeen. Following his discharge in the fall of 1945, he entered Prairie View A&M College. Upon graduation he received his teaching certificate, and like Don Terry, began a thirty-six-year career in the public school system at Chester, Texas, the hometown of his wife. He retired as principal of the public high school a few years ago and still resides in Chester, Texas.

Leon Netka, who served as a radioman, following discharge moved from Hearne, Texas, his hometown, to Houston and began a career in the accounting department of a major oil company based in Houston. At age sixty-five he retired and recently moved back to Hearne, Texas.

A. L. Womack, who was a radioman on the ship, returned to Star City, Arkansas, after discharge. He later moved to Pine Bluff and is now retired, like most everyone else who served on the *SC-761* in World War II.

Joseph E. Vandergriff, who served in the engineering gang on board the *SC-761*, returned to Alton, Illinois, after discharge. He later moved to New Jersey, where he worked for a chemical company. Recently, he passed away and his widow, Jean, still resides in North Plainfield, New Jersey.

George H. Haigwood, GM2/c, after discharge in November 1945, returned to Arkansas. He began work for a trucking company. His cousin, Catherine Haigwood, of Clarksville, Arkansas, his hometown, reported to me that he died in 1961 when his large eighteen-wheeler truck jackknifed.

Paul B. Pullen, who also served as a radioman, returned to his hometown of Clewiston, Florida, following discharge. He, too, has recently died.

Your author reported to SCTC in March 1943 for advanced training. Although assigned to the DE Command School, I hoped to obtain duty on something larger than a PC or DE. My often queasy stomach desired a larger ship. One officer on the assignment committee at SCTC was a friend who had been two classes ahead of me at Amherst College. Another fellow Amherst man was on the cruiser desk at BuPers. Through their efforts I was able to obtain orders to the USS *Richmond* (CL-9), flagship of CruDiv One and of the North Pacific Task Force. After participating in bombardments of northern Japanese islands, the *Richmond* took part in the initial occupation of Japan. In this regard it led elements of the North Pacific Fleet into Ominato Harbor, where Vice Adm. Frank Jack Fletcher accepted the surrender of the the Ominato Naval Reservation, Northern Honshu and the island of Hokaido.

I served on the *Richmond* until it was decommissioned in December 1945. Released to inactive duty in early 1946, I entered law school at The University of Texas at Austin. Following graduation, I was selected for the one-year appointment as briefing attorney (law clerk) to the Chief Justice of the Texas Supreme Court, the late John E. Hickman. Afterwards I came to Abilene, Texas, to practice law, retiring in 1986. Now I am adjunct professor of legal studies at McMurry University in Abilene, Texas. Remaining active in the U.S. Naval Reserve, I retired as a captain in 1971.

After being decommissioned, the *SC-761* was stricken from the navy register on 19 December 1945. Subsequently, it was transferred to the Maritime Commission in early 1948, which thereupon delivered it to Crowley Launch & Tugboat Company, purchaser at the U.S. Naval Magazine, Port Chicago, California. I have not been able to determine how or where it may have been used thereafter.

The W. A. Robinson Shipyard at Ipswich, Massachusetts, had a somewhat similar inconspicuous ending to that of the *USS SC-761*. Today, it would take a very careful search to locate any of its remnants. With both World War II and Robinson's marriage at an end, he abandoned the yard which had been his dream. Embarking on his elegant, modern schooner, the *Varuna*, which had been built under his personal supervision, he sailed, alone, to Tahiti to spend the rest of his life. Gauguin, deja vu!

In 1972 the *Ipswich Chronicle* published a series of articles concerning Robinson and his former shipyard. In the final installment published on 6 April 1972, the newspaper concluded:

> Suddenly it was all over, the war, the yard, everything. Mr. Robinson sailed away to Tahiti leaving . . . others to pick up and dispose of the pieces. And what pieces! Ten or a dozen buildings crammed with surplus, bronze fittings and valves, fastenings, tools, enough to stock a marine hardware store for five years, but all bought on high priority, now worth only their value as scrap metal. It was carried away by the truckload, and finally the buildings, too, were knocked down and hauled away. The men of the yard scattered to the four winds, the bulldozers covered every trace and only the seagulls remain.

Appendices

APPENDIX A
ORIGINAL CREW AT TIME OF COMMISSIONING

Officers:

Lt. (jg) F. D. ANDRUS — Commanding Officer
Ens. A. W. McGUIRE — Executive Officer

Crew:

Name	Rating
GALFORD, D. B.	CBM
CEBULA, E.	GM1c
BUKOCY, A.	QM2c
BUDZISZ, J. A.	SM2c
TARASZKA, T. J.	EM2c
WILLIAMS, A. B., Jr.	Y2c
RYAN, W. J.	RM1c
LACY, J. J.	RM3c
WOOTTEN, G. E.	SoM3c
COOGAN, J. J.	SC1c
JOHNSON, J. P.	MA2c
SOUTHWICK, K. W. B.	MoMM1c
RANNEY, M. A.	MoMM2c
GROVE, A. S.	MoMM2c
HARTMANN, R. J.	MoMM2c
SINGER, N. A.	MoMM3c
McMULLEN, D. L.	F2c
BOK, T.	S1c(GM)
JAMES, M. D.	S1c
PULLEN, P. B.	S1c(RM)

APPENDIX B
CREW DEPARTING BALBOA FOR SOUTH PACIFIC

Officers:

Lt. (jg) RONALD B. BALCOM — Commanding Officer

Ens. J. HENRY DOSCHER, JR. — Executive Officer

Ens. JAMES B. HANNAH — Third Officer

Crew:

Name	Rating
GALFORD, D. B.	CBM
TARASZKA, T. J.	EM1c
BURRELL, G. A.	QM2c
BUDZISZ, J. A.	SM2c
CHOINSKI, C. J. "SKI"	GM2c
BOK, T.	GM2c
HIGHTOWER, F. E.	SoM2c
WOOTTEN, G. E.	SoM3c
TERRY, D. N.	Y3c
WASLOUSKY, A. J.	RM2c
PULLEN, P. B.	RM3c
SANSFACON, A. J. "FRENCHIE"	SC2c
JOHNSON, J. P. "WILLIE"	MA2c
GARDINER, C. A.	RdM3c
HARTMANN, R. J. "RUDY"	MoMM1c
GROVE, A. S.	MoMM2c
SINGER, N. A., JR.	MoM2c
HAWKINS, R. D.	MoMM2c
McMULLEN, D. L.	F1c
VANDERGRIFF, J. E.	F2c
WEST, GEO. L.	COX
MOORE, JAS. T.	S2c
GRIMM, R. S.	S2c
GROESCHEL, J. M.	S2c

APPENDIX C
CREW RETURNING SHIP TO SAN FRANCISCO

Officers:
 Lt. (jg) JOHN O'B. ELFELT — Commanding Officer
 Ens. JAMES T. MADDOX — Executive Officer
 Ens. WARREN A. MILLER — Third Officer

Crew:

Name	*Rating*
O'DAY, J. J.	BM2c
HAIGWOOD, G. H.	GM2c
MIKLOS, R. A.	SoM2c
SPEEG, J. K.	EM2c
ROSTKOWSKI, J. S.	SC2c
BEARD, V. G.	Y3c
HEDEGAARD, H. W.	QM3c
HECK, J. B.	QM3c
BUCHER, J. O.	RM3c
COLE, C. F., JR.	RM3c
CARPENTER, F. C.	MoMM2c
RICE, G. R.	MoMM2c
DASSATTI, R. A.	MoMM3c
EVANS, E. J.	MoMM3c
CHASE, R. G.	COX
KOPYCINSKI, E. J.	COX
WARKENTINE, O. R.	COX
McLAUGHLIN, F. A.	S1c

Passenger:
 ENS. FLOYD T. GATES

APPENDIX D

SOME NOTES OF LIEUTENANT ROBINSON McILVAINE, ES-CORT COMMANDER, IN THE WAR DIARY OF USS *SC-730*, AT BORA BORA REGARDING THE VOYAGE FROM BALBOA.

10 March 1943:

At 1640 anchored in fourteen fathoms of water in Tevenui Bay, BoraBora, with *SCs 761* and *641* nested on either side.

NOTES ON VOYAGE FROM BALBOA

The voyage just completed was one of the longest ever undertaken by so many small craft together. The fact that so long a voyage should be completed, literally without incident, is in no small measure due to the careful preparations made before sailing. Over a period of ten days prior to departure the convoy and escort commanders held daily conferences to work out all the details of fueling and provisions at sea, communications, sound and radar search, and systematic rotation of screening vessels.

Because the LCI(L)s have a cruising radius of approximately 10,000 miles it was anticipated that most difficulties in the way of breakdown, etc., would originate among the Submarine Chasers and the Mine Sweepers. Accordingly the PECOS carried as passengers a group of diesel, radar, and sound experts to assist in any repairs which might be necessary enroute. The actual performance of the various type vessels proved to be the reverse of what was expected.

A number of LCI(L)s, two mine sweepers, and even the PECOS had to be taken in tow at one time or another. There were no casualties whatsoever among the Submarine Chasers. While no great significance is claimed for this performance, it is felt that the excellent training which submarine chaser officers and men receive at the S.C.T.C., Miami, Florida, had something to do with it.

Actually the performance of the LCI(L)s was no less than amazing considering the fact that few had any higher ratings than SM3/c, and most of the officers saw salt water for the first time when they departed Galveston, Texas, a few weeks before. On this voyage and what was to follow they learned navigation, seamanship, and engineering the hard way.

Fueling at sea was accomplished with a minimum of difficulty. Every third or fourth day, depending on weather conditions, each submarine chaser and mine sweeper went alongside the PECOS at the convoy speed of the moment — sometimes 10, sometimes 12 knots. In general the whole procedure of taking fuel, water, and provisions required only forty to fifty minutes.

APPENDIX E
A REPORT INVOLVING TYPICAL HAZARDS ENCOUN-
TERED BY SUBCHASERS OPERATING IN THE
SOLOMON ISLANDS
(Originally Secret, Now Declassified)

Action Report

USS *SC-505*
SeriaL 12   31 August 1943

Battle Action Of USS *SC-505*, Report Of.

Report Covers Action Off Barakoma, Vella Lavella
During Air Attack By 35 Enemy Planes, 6 Of Which
Attacked This Ship. *SC-505* Received Extensive
Damage To The Sound Gear And Electrical System
As A Result Of 5 Near Misses, On 21 August 1943.

USS SUB CHASER 505

SC-505
A16-3(12)
S E C R E T   31 August 1943
From :   The Commanding Officer.
To :   Commander in Chief, U.S. Pacific Fleet
Via :   (1) Commander Task Group 31.7
                (2) Commander Task Force 31
                (3) Commander South Pacific Forces
Subject: Battle Action of USS *SC-505*, Report of.
Reference: (a) U.S. Navy Regulations, Article 712 and 874(6).

1. Report in accordance with reference (a) is hereby submitted.

2. On the morning of 21 August 1943, this vessel, un-accom-
panied, was conducting screening operations three thousand yards
off Barakoma, Vella Lavella Island, where *LSTs 354, 395,* and *398*
were unloading men and supplies.

3. Ship's radio was guarding assigned frequency of 3000 Kcs.,
and wardroom radio was tuned to fighter control frequency. At 1000,
warning was received that 35 enemy planes were approaching Vella
Gulf. The ship was then on course 010 degrees (T). At 1010, enemy
planes were sighted over Vella Lavella Island bearing 270 degrees (T).
As our fighters closed to intercept, six Aichi type 99 Dive Bombers
began their dive and attacked this ship, coming in on the port quarter. Five bombs were dropped, landing at distances of from 20 to 40

feet off the quarter, one off the beam, and one broad on the bow. All dive bombers strafed the ship during the attack. The near misses caused extensive damage to the sound gear and the electrical system.

4. Approximately 40 rounds of 40 MM, 110 rounds of 20 MM, and 200 rounds of 30 Cal. ammunition were fired at the attacking planes. The last dive bomber was reported to be smoking just prior to releasing its bomb.

5. The last bomb dropped at a distance of 20 feet from the port bow and caused the ship to heel over to a 65 degree angle. Water flooded the deck to a depth of 24 inches. Two of the three 20 MM ready boxes were completely inundated and all ordnance equipment topside was soaked with salt water spray.

6. One man received a shrapnel injury and is still undergoing medical treatment. Minor injuries were suffered by the officers and men as a result of being thrown about the ship.

7. The conduct of the officers and men during the attack was highly commendable. Especially deserving of recognition are: Kuzmak, Michael Jr., MoMM1c, Crump, Glen O. EM1c, and Paisley, James R. GM2c.

8. Screening operations were continued at 1020, damage to sound gear not being discovered until arrival at base.

J. M. Nagle

❖ ❖ ❖

LSTFLOT5/A16-3

LST FLOTILLA FIVE
AMPHIBIOUS FORCE, SOUTH PACIFIC

S E C R E T   5 SEPTEMBER 1943

First Endorsement To
USS *SC-505* Secret
Serial 12 of 31 August 1943

From: The Commander Task Group 31.7
To   :   The Commander in Chief, U.S. Pacific Fleet
Via :   (1) The Commander Task Group 31.1
             (2) The Commander Task Force 31
             (3) The Commander South Pacific Force
Subject: Battle Action of USS *SC-505*, Report of.
Reference: (a) ComTaskGroup 31.7 SECRET Serial 0140 of 5 September 1943.

1. Forwarded.

2. Attention is invited to Paragraph 3 of reference (a) which indicates the desirability of having such type accompany a convoy in submarine waters where plane attacks are to be expected.

3. The Group Commander notes with pleasure the commendable conduct indicated in Paragraph 8 of the basic report on the part of Michael J. Kuzmak, MoMM1c, Glen O. Crump, EM1c, and James R. Paisley, GM2c, and takes the opportunity to congratulate them.

G. B. Carter

Copy to:
    ComINCH (Advance Copy)
    USS SC-505

❖ ❖ ❖

S-E-C-R-E-T   12 September 1943
SECOND ENDORSEMENT To
USS SC-505 SECRET
Serial 12 of 31 August 1943.

From: The Commander Task Group 31.1.
To   :   The Commander in Chief, U. S. Pacific Fleet.
Via   :   (1) The Commander Task Group 31.1
            (2) The Commander Task Force 31.
            (3) The Commander South Pacific Force.
Subject: Battle Action of USS *SC-505*, Report of.
Reference: (a) ComTaskGroup 31.7 SECRET Serial 0140 of 5 September 1943.

1. Forwarded.

2. Commander Task Group 31.7 was under the operational control of Commander Task Force 31 during this action.

G. H. Fort

❖ ❖ ❖

THIRD AMPHIBIOUS FORCE
Office of the Commander
Serial 00385

05/Do
17 September 1943

S-E-C-R-E-T
THIRD ENDORSEMENT to
USS SC-505 secret ltr
serial 12 dated 31 August 1943.

From: Commander Task Force Thirty-One.
To   :   Commander-in-Chief, U.S. Pacific Fleet
Via   :   Commander South Pacific.
Subject: Battle Action of USS *SC-505*, Report of.

    1. Forwarded. The spirited defense of this small vessel alone against a heavy dive-bombing attack is highly commendable.

    2. In this instance, as in other *Barakoma* convoys, the destroyers were withdrawn during the unloading period of the LST's, and the SC left as a screen against possible submarine attack on the beached LST's. This deprives the SC of the benefit of the destroyers' anti-aircraft fire, but is done in order to remove the larger and more valuable combatant vessels from the usual air attack following close upon the arrival of the convoy. Heavy air-cover is provided during the unloading period but it is to be expected that some dive-bombers may get through.

T. S. Wilkinson

Copy to:
    CTG 31.1
    CTG 31.7
    CO USS SC-505

❖ ❖ ❖

SOUTH PACIFIC FORCE
of the United States Pacific Fleet
Headquarters of the Commander

ComSoPac File:
A16-3/(90)
Serial 002028
S-E-C-R-E-T   4 October 1943
FOURTH ENDORSEMENT to
USS SC-505 secret ltr
Serial 12 dated 31 August 1943.
From: The Commander South Pacific.
To   :   The Commander in Chief, U.S. Pacific Fleet
Subject: Battle Action of USS SC-505, Report of.
    1. Forwarded.

I. H. Mayfiel, Acting Chief of Staff

Copy to:
    CTF 31
    CTG 31.1
    Com LST Flot 5
    CO SC-505

Author's Note

In addition to the data in the bibliography, the following research information is provided.

Personal Interviews

With various former members of ship's company, including: Ronald B. Balcom of Palm Beach, Florida, and Fishers Island, New York; James B. Hannah of Minneapolis, Minnesota; Joseph F. Effinger of Fort Lauderdale, Florida; Don W. Terry of Miami, Florida; George A. Burrell of Jensen Beach, Florida, and Long Island, New York; and Leon Netka of Houston, Texas. Former Solomon Islands coastwatcher Martin Clemens of Dunraven, Toorak, Victoria, Australia.

Telephone Interviews and Correspondence

With the above former members of ship's company, together with: James T. Moore of Lynchburg, Virginia; Marson W. Pierce of Gunnison, Colorado; John O'Brien Elfelt of Anoka, Minnesota; Julius Plato Johnson of Chester, Texas; Warner Keeley, Jr., of Pebble Beach, California; Col. Herbert E. Holliday USA (Ret.) of Carlisle, Pennsylvania; and Ms. Natalie Anderson, reference librarian, Ipswich Public Library, Ipswich, Massachusetts.

Correspondence Only

With Rear Adm. Norvell G. Ward of Atlantic Beach, Florida; A. L. Womak of Pine Bluff, Arkansas; Harvey Hedegaard of Lucedale, Mississippi; Kenneth M. Gordon, Spartanburg, South Carolina; and Lt. Comdr. John R. Keenan, Royal Australian Navy (Ret.) of Nambour, Queensland, Australia.

Official Records

The log books, war diaries, and/or action reports located in Washington, D.C., at the National Archives on Pennsylvania Avenue and the U.S. Naval Historical Center at the Washington Navy Yard regarding various

United States Navy ships, including: *SCs 505, 514, 518, 641, 648, 698, 700, 701, 730, 739, 751, 760, 761, 981,* and *982*; USS *Cony* (DD-508); USS *Guardfish* (SS-217).

The ship's roster for USS *SC-761* located at the National Archives.

Marine charts of South Pacific areas during the World War II era. These charts are located in the Arlington, Virginia, Annex of the National Archives, and include chart numbers 2016, 2850, 2864, 2865, 2896, 2918, 2920, and 5905.

Photographs

Those of the above persons who furnished photographs in their possession include: Ronald B. Balcom; James B. Hannah; Don W. Terry; James O'Brien Elfelt; Marson W. Pierce; Warner Keeley, Jr.; and author.

Poet

The author has not been able to uncover any information concerning Oris E. Moore, the composer of the poem "The Splinter Fleet." A recent detailed inquiry by research librarians failed to uncover anything published by him at any time. A typed, carbon copy of such poem was uncovered in the dusty navy files of James B. Hannah. The best recollections are that carbon copies of this poem circulated among various ships of the Splinter Fleet in the South Pacific. Fortunately, one of those copies was saved by Mr. Hannah, a meticulous, Harvard-trained attorney of Minneapolis. This poem so well describes the conditions endured by the crews of subchasers, as well as their high spirits, Mr. Oris E. Moore surely served on board such a ship during World War II. Wherever he may be, the author is proud to credit Mr. Moore with this poetic endeavor.

Bibliography

Only through extensive research of records in the National Archives and in the U.S. Naval Historical Center, and by contacting and interviewing former officers and crewmen who served on the *SC-761*, have I been able to write this saga. When I left the ship at Suva in February 1944, I took with me the names and home addresses of each person aboard the ship. Some I have stayed in contact with over these many years. Others I began searching for in the spring of 1990. Those men who were originally from small towns were easier to locate, as I wrote or called every person with that last name in the current telephone directory. Often I reached a cousin or other relative who either put me in touch with a former shipmate, or reported his death. A now retired New York City attorney was located through assistance of the State Bar of New York.

After three years and much correspondence, I was able to obtain recollections of many former members of ship's company. That has not been an easy job, as privacy regulations now prevent governmental bureaus from furnishing assistance in locating people. Although significant changes of personnel occurred regularly, and no one person served on the ship from beginning to end, I did locate, contact, and interview someone from each segment of the ship's history. As a result of my personal sleuthing, I obtained eyewitness accounts of all events from the day the commission pennant was first raised to the time it was hauled down for the last time. I was able to interview, sometimes in person, sometimes by telephone, every former commanding officer except the very first one. All of this served to verify and amplify data I obtained from official records. Such contacts prompted the recovery of old photographs, as well as a sketch of the USS *SC-761* drawn by one of its former crewmen while overseas.

105

I was able to locate in Atlantic Beach, Florida, the former commanding officer of the SS *Guardfish*. In 1943 he was known to me as Comdr. Norvell G. Ward; now he is a retired rear admiral. He was kind enough to write and confirm our experiences in the Solomon Islands, particularly the removal of coastwatchers from Bougainville.

When he was in San Antonio, Texas, for an Admiral Nimitz Foundation Symposium, I was able to personally interview Mr. Martin Clemens now of Dunraven, Toorak, Victoria, Australia. Following his graduation from Cambridge University, Mr. Clemens joined the Bristish Foreign Service and was posted to the Solomon Islands immediately prior to the outbreak of World War II. He became one of the celebrated Solomon Islands coastwatchers of Guadalcanal and New Georgia.

By correspondence, I have exchanged information with Lt. Comdr. John R. Keenan, Royal Australian Navy, V.G. (Ret.), now of Nambour, Queensland, Australia. He was the leader of the first group of Bougainville coastwatchers the USS *SC-761* returned to Guadalcanal. He refreshed my memory of some details of that operation.

Among the subchasers, the USS *SC-641* operated with us extensively, and I located in Pebble Beach, California, one of its former officers, Warner Keeley, Jr. He and his subchaser were with us from Miami until we departed the Solomons for duty out of Suva, and his recollections and some photographs have been very helpful.

For the precise data, I reviewed the log books, war diaries and action reports, all now declassified, of navy ships of all types with which the *SC-761* served at various times. These official records are located either in the National Archives on Pennsylvania Avenue or the Naval Historical Center at the Washington Navy Yard. It took two long trips to Washington, D.C., to research and obtain that information, as well as to review and copy old navigation charts from the WWII era located in the Arlington, Virginia, annex of the archives. To the best of my ability this story of the *SC-761* is accurate. Of course, I personally experienced thirteen critical months of this saga as a young officer and many of the events are indelibly etched in my mind.

In recent years I thought something should be presented about this unsung portion of the navy as to its operations in the Pacific theater of military operations. By this book I have attempted to make a small but accurate contribution, hopefully interesting, in that respect.

Index